AF064188

LOVE
against
the
LAW

The autobiographies of Tex and Nelly Camfoo

Readers should be aware that if members of some Aboriginal communities see the names or images of the deceased, particularly their relatives, they may be distressed.

Before using this book in such communities, the wishes of senior members should be established and their advice taken on appropriate procedures and safeguards.

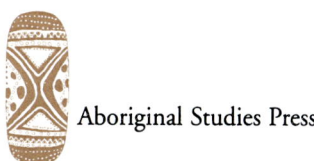

Aboriginal Studies Press

FIRST PUBLISHED IN 2000 by
Aboriginal Studies Press
For the Australian Institute of Aboriginal and Torres Strait Islander Studies
GPO Box 553 Canberra ACT 2601

Acknowledgement:
The authors and publisher wish to acknowledge with thanks the financial contribution to this publication by the University of Technology, Sydney.

The views expressed in this publication are those of the author and not necessarily those of the Australian Institute of Aboriginal and Torres Strait Islander Studies.

© Tex Camfoo, Nelly Camfoo and Gillian Cowlishaw 2000

The publisher has made every effort to contact copyright owners for permission to use material reproduced in this book. If your material has been used inadvertently without permission, please contact the publisher immediately.

Apart from any fair dealing for the purpose of private study, research, criticism or review, as permitted under the Copyright Act, no part of this publication may be reproduced by any process whatsoever without the written permission of the publisher.

NATIONAL LIBRARY OF AUSTRALIA CATALOGUING-IN-PUBLICATION DATA

Camfoo, Tex.
Love against the law : the autobiographies of Tex and Nelly Camfoo.

ISBN 0 85575 348 X

1. Camfoo, Tex. 2. Camfoo, Nelly. 3. Aborigines, Australian — Northern Territory — Social conditions — 20th century — Biography. 4. Aborigines, Australian — Legal status, laws, etc. — Northern Territory. 5. Country life — Northern Territory — Anecdotes. 6. Australia — Race relations. I. Cowlishaw, Gillian K. (Gillian Keir), 1934– . II. Camfoo, Nelly. III. Title.

920.00929915

PRODUCED BY	Aboriginal Studies Press
EDITING AND DESIGN BY	Themeda
PHOTOGRAPHS	Dodd collection Museum and Art Gallery of the Northern Territory, Gillian Cowlishaw, Charles Chauvel, Cornelia Vervoorn, Hal Wootten
PRINTED IN AUSTRALIA BY	Ligare Pty Ltd, Riverwood, NSW

2000/1/2000

CONTENTS

Preface		v
1.	My mother, Florida	1
2.	Groote Eylandt	4
3.	Roper Mission	8
4.	Treacle	11
5.	Bush tucker	13
6.	Running away	16
7.	The big flood	20
8.	That was the copper!	23
9.	Missionaries	25
10.	Girlfriends	29
	1. Leaving Arnhem Land, finding Mainoru	32
11.	Horses	35
	2. Hard work	38
12.	Number two war	40
	3. War	42
13.	Elsey	43
14.	George Conway	46
15.	Mainoru, murders and memories	50
	4. They savvy our life	56
16.	Just roosting marriage	58
	5. 'You can't take that girl'	61
17.	White or black?	62
18.	My old dad, Jimmy Camfoo	66
19.	Permission to marry	72
	6. Love and marriage	74

20.	The dog ticket	76
21.	Stockmen and landowners	78
22.	Rodeo and races	80
23.	Whitefella, blackfella?	82
24.	Christmas	83
25.	Poddy dodging	86
26.	Leaving Mainoru	89
	7. They didn't want blackfella	92
27.	Managing Gulperan Pastoral Company	94
28.	The saddlery	99
29.	Young people	101
30.	Gods	104
	8. Women's centre	106
	9. I didn't get my culture from Mr Keating	107
	10. Voting	110
	11. We dusted them up	112
	12. Money in stones	114
	References	116
	Postscript	117

PREFACE

The autobiographies of Tex and Nelly Camfoo show how they dealt with the peculiar race relations which existed in the Northern Territory. Tex was variously defined as Aboriginal, half-caste and European at different times in his life. Nelly was always Aboriginal, written as *aboriginal* for many years. Other common vernacular terms included part-coloured, yellafella, and half-breed for Tex; myall, lubra, native and full-blood for Nelly. Now they are both Aboriginal, officially at least.

Tex was born near Roper River in the Northern Territory in about 1922. He is the son of Jimmy Camfoo, a Chinese saddler, and Florida, a Rembarrnga woman. At the time the social position of what were known as 'mixed blood' or 'half-caste' people was unstable and unpredictable. No firm legal status existed in between *black* and *white*; an individual was either subject to the *Aboriginal Ordinance 1918* or not. Under this Commonwealth ordinance the Northern Territory's Native Affairs Branch expended a great deal of time and energy deciding who was and who was not subject to its provisions. Even though identified as Aboriginal, Tex's appearance determined his fate and as a small boy he was taken away to the half-caste school at Groote Eylandt and later placed in the mission dormitory at Roper. The missionaries were not always virtuous and the police not always lawful, but Tex shows that he can appreciate their temptations. He even called one policeman his stepfather.

During his working life on various cattle stations, Tex adopted the popular cowboy style of the outback stockmen, including the name 'Tex'. The labour of skilled stockmen was valued, but Tex was only allowed to enter the pub with his white mates when given an exemption certificate or when reclassified as European. Tex' marriages were also complicated by the contradictory rules of white law and missionary practice. Tex' final reflections on the morality and meaning of racial difference reveals a religious imagination and a sense of history which stem from a life on the racial borderlands.

Nelly is also a reflective person and her comments on whitefellas are both ironic and insightful. She was born in Arnhem Land around 1932 and recalls how sorry she was for the first Europeans she saw. The intrusion of white people was a challenge to which Nelly responded with enthusiasm. She has never allowed their presence to humiliate her as it did some who were perhaps more sensitive. She finds white people at once frustrating and foolish, and believes they cannot understand because they cannot listen. With little opportunity to become literate, she has often said 'If I'd learned to read and write I'd have had a good job like you.' I have no doubt that she would have had a far more significant role in the world than mine were she literate.

I met Tex and Nelly when I began research at Bulman in 1975. Tex was then the Aboriginal manager of the Gulperan Pastoral Company, a cattle venture funded in the early days of the policy of Aboriginal self-determination which was intended to allow communities to control their own lives by managing their affairs. There was a white manager as well, and the workers were mainly Rembarrnga stockmen previously of Mainoru cattle station, from which they had been ejected when Aborigines had to be paid equal wages. The new American owner of Mainoru had not wanted the 'black's camp' to remain with 'a lot of unnecessary people', so the families had, in 1969, taken their goats and swags and walked off the station to the Arnhem Land Reserve. Thus ended a sixty year association, and the 'Mainoru mob' became the 'Bulman mob'. Initially they had built bush houses at Bigetti and lived on bush tucker, but the Welfare Branch of the Commonwealth department moved them to Gonjimbi where there were some old tin huts and shacks left over from a small mining venture, and where they could be provided with rations.

When I arrived in 1975 this place was called Bulman and the housing had been supplemented with a caravan for the white manager, some canvas, and sheets of blue plastic and roofing iron. The supply of water and electricity came from hoses and cords which snaked across the camp in all directions. I was particularly conscious of these material conditions because my research project in 1975 and 1976 mainly involved women and children. While camping out during the dry season in the Territory is far from arduous, I did sometimes wish I had brought with me the proverbial kitchen sink instead of anthropology books.

Nelly looked after my welfare from the beginning and she was always ready to talk and discuss a whole range of matters. Nelly's story is an edited version of recordings made between 1975 and 1993 in the camp or the bush, and once at the *Djarada* ceremony grounds. Nelly added more when I read the narrative to her in 1993.

Tex was at first suspicious of anthropologists, although after I returned for the second visit, he invited me to ride his old stock-horse, Silver. But it was not until 1993 that Tex agreed to tape-record an account of his life. He did so with much enthusiasm and we sat for many hours as he wove the account backwards and forwards through adventures and reflections, recounting the excitement, humour and suffering of his life. He was delighted with the transcribed and re-ordered text which I took to Bulman in 1995 for him to read. That year, and again in 1997, he described some more recent events and expanded on his beliefs about the Bible, Christianity and Aborigines, and his anxieties about young people and the Aboriginal future.

While most of the text has been edited into standard English at the direction of Tex and Nelly, I have tried to keep the rhythm of their fluent and colourful speech. Also there are some non-standard or ambiguous usages that contain meanings that are important to the narrative. In particular, Tex sometimes uses *they* alternating with *we* when he is speaking of Aboriginal people, illustrating that the cultural borderlands which he inhabits can sometimes be a no-man's land. Other non-standard usages are from the local Kriol—linguistically a creole language—which combines elements of English with local Aboriginal languages. Kriol is widely recognised and, with its own orthography, is used in some schools in the Northern Territory.

It took many years for Tex to trust me enough to record his biography. One reason is to do with kinship and normal practices of avoidance between siblings. As among Aborigines generally, everyone at Bulman stands in some kind of kin relationship to everyone else and like all who live in such a community, I was given a kinship designation (subsection *Ngaritjan*) which placed me within these family relationships. Each relationship entails certain obligations and expectations. I became a 'sister' (*yabok*) to Lorna Martin and Jill Curtis and 'mother' (*mula*) to their children. To Nelly I became a specific kind of 'cousin' (*bunji*), and an Aunty to those she called daughter or son. Tex' subsection is *Ngaridj* so he is my classificatory 'brother', and the duty of avoidance between brothers and sisters among Rembarrnga people placed a barrier against our talking together. While Tex saw my kin obligations as ambiguous and even voluntary because I am a whitefella, the attaining of more advanced years has made it easier for us to sit together and exchange stories.

Gillian Cowlishaw

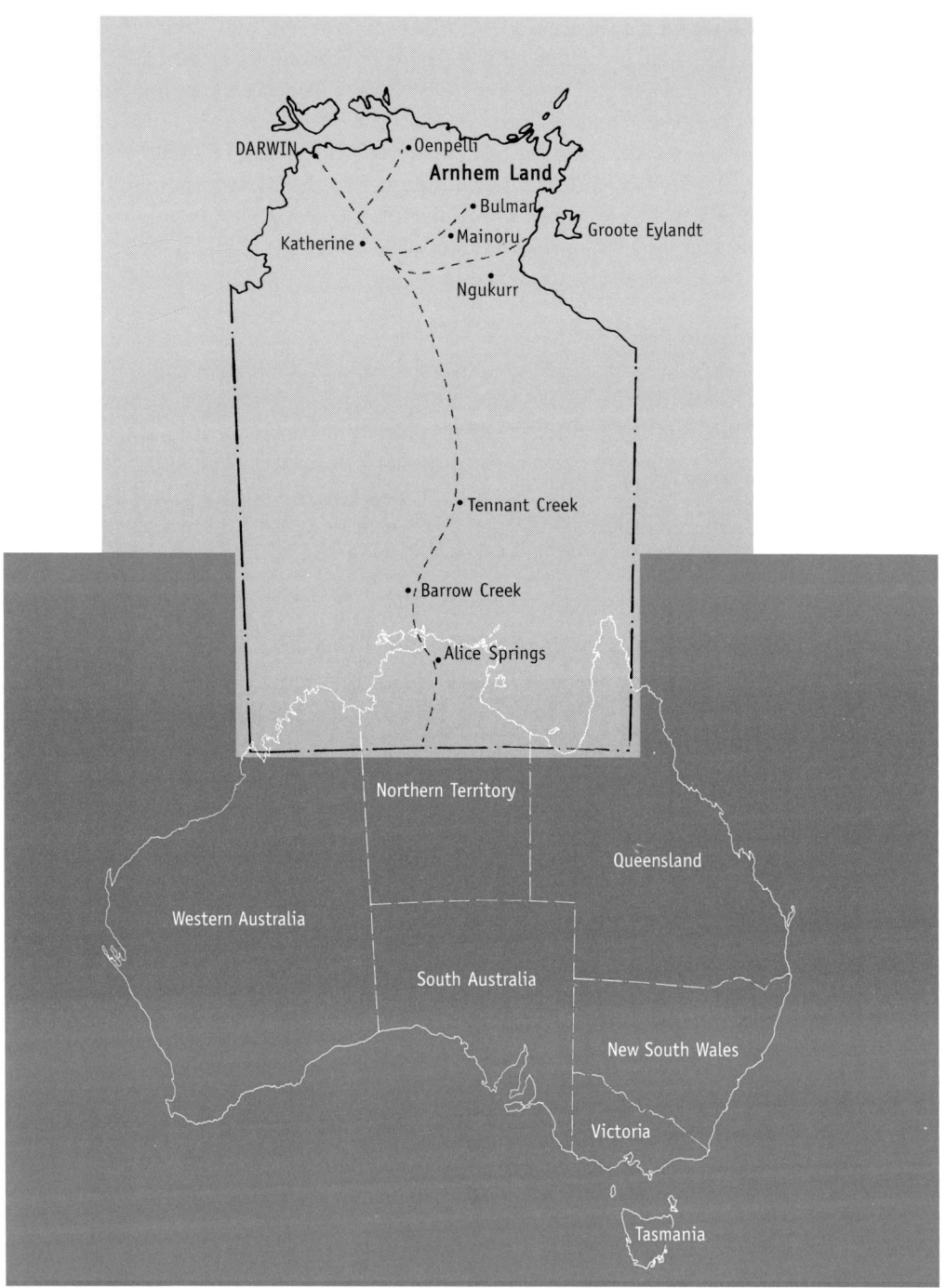

1. MY MOTHER, FLORIDA

I was born in the camp.

My mother was Florida. When my sister was born, probably a couple of days after, some white men raided our camp and they killed my sister. They grabbed her by the leg and banged her up against the tree. And my Aunty Edna, *Niluk,* she got me and ran away in the hills with me.

In those days when there were half-caste, they used to kill us you know because they reckon we different colour to the other Aboriginal people. But my Aunty Edna said,

'No, you can't kill this little boy. He's my little boy. And he's going to spear kangaroo and fish and get sugarbag [honey] and look after me when he grows up.'

Anyway, we walked around, all over that place. Right down to Jim Jim, through Mary River and Alligator River, all through Oenpelli. There was no towns. Katherine was just nothing yet. From place to place we used to walk around. Never mind where we go, we used to end up back at Roper Valley or up in Roper Bar.

Then that old mission, old Roper River mission, CMS came. They started to get all the young people, all the little people, all the children from all over the place, to start a school there, to teach them about Christianity and all that. I was still walking around with my mother, out in the bush. My mother used to take

The Roper area

Roper Bar was originally the police station. In 1908 the Church Missionary Society (CMS) established a mission on the site. After being washed away in floods in the 1940s the settlement was moved upstream to the Roper River Mission at the place now called Ngukurr.

In 1921 the CMS established a school for half-caste children on Groote Eylandt just off the coast.

Roper Valley and Urapunga are local cattle stations where Tex worked.

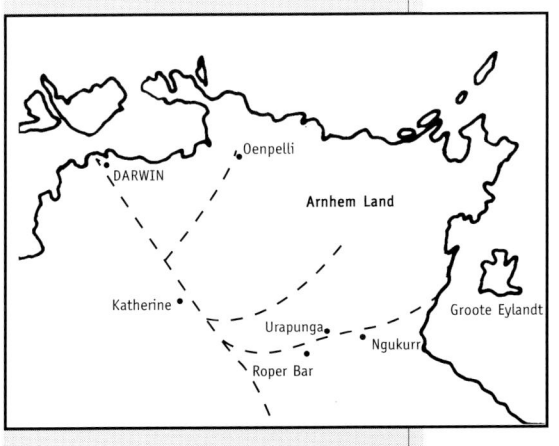

me out with my [step]father Power Jack and he started to teach me blackfella way.

The white men tried to shoot Aboriginal people out. Because they were in good country I suppose, because they wanted it for themselves. They would try to find where they got a big camp, or ceremony. My old stepfather, Power Jack, was a blacktracker. He used to go and tell them 'Big mob of them there'. But he checked up on me first. I was only about this high. They used to take me up the hills then. Mum Florida, Aunty Edna. They'd take me up in the caves and plant me there. We'd hear the bang, bang, going on everywhere, poor things.

One day they came up there. My stepfather was there and we kids were playing around looking for tobacco and we found a revolver wrapped up in the swag. He said,

> 'Come on run away now. Take this boy up in the hills. *Mununga* [whitefella] going to come directly.'

They took me up in the hills and they took the revolver too. My stepfather must have looked for it I suppose and never found it. He didn't say anything. Power Jack would take me out in the bush for four or five months and then they'd go somewhere for a ceremony and his brother, old Yarramanek, would look after me for a while.

My mother used to come up to Roper Valley station and get some tobacco and sugar and things and take me away in the bush again. She was quite aware of things. She knew the white man might want to take the yellafellas [half-castes] away. Power Jack knew, they all knew. They used to find out when they were working as stockmen.

Family

Tex uses the term *stepfather* for his 'social' rather than his 'biological' father, but many Aboriginal people would also extend the term *father* to 'father's brother' or to 'mother's husband' and *mother* can refer to 'mother's sisters'.

Tex' biological father, Jimmy Camfoo, wasn't around a great deal during Tex' childhood.

Frontier violence

Aborigines' stories of the early days of white settlement are full of bloodshed as well as intimacy between white and black people.

Power Jack's protection of his stepson when he betrayed the position of the camp reflects a set of local circumstances rather than general conditions on the frontier (see Mickey Dewar, *The 'Black War' in Arnhem Land*, 1992).

Racial terminology

Tex uses racial language that may seem shocking to some readers, but this was ordinary language in his youth. Even today, the usual Northern Territory terminology defines people in racial terms: *whites, half-castes, blackfellas*.

Tex' use of *we* and *they* when referring to his family or other Aboriginal people indicates his ambiguous racial position, especially his acceptance in the social world of white stockmen, among whom his Aboriginality was muted and could be ignored.

'We've got to take away that boy now. White man might take him away now.'

Because they knew that white men didn't like the half-caste. Kids, you know, from the white man. We were outcasts because they didn't like us. But thanks to my mother and stepfather, they'd take me out in the scrub and live in a cave there for a few days. My stepfather, Power Jack, would go in and find out and he'd say, 'Everything is all right now.' So we'd go in and get some tobacco for him and away we'd go again.

My old stepfather grew me up, he said to me, 'About time you should go back there to school. Go to school, down Roper River.'

So we packed all our gear and packed all our swags, spears and things, and we walked from Roper Valley down to Roper Bar.

I was somewhere about four, five years old when we went down there. There used to be coppers there, policemen. Like Frank Stretton. He was one of my stepfathers. Well, I used to call him stepfather. I used to play with him and he'd feed us and look after us and all.

Old Barnabas Roper, he come over with his wife, and Phillip and Silas Roberts. They were all little kids. I was bigger than them. They come and pick me up and took me down to Roper River. They put me in a school there. Mum used to come up and see me sometimes, but when I gradually grew up, about two-three years after, they sent all the half-caste people to Groote Eylandt then.

Sexual laws and relationships

The exchange of sexual favours for food, tobacco and other material goods was a common trading practice on Australia's racial frontiers. However under the *Aboriginal Ordinance (1918)* it was an offence for a white man to 'unlawfully have carnal knowledge of a female Aborigine or half-caste' and in 1936 it became an offence for a white male 'to live or cohabit or have sexual intercourse with any Aborigine or half-caste not his lawful wife (penalty £100 or six months gaol or both)'.

2. GROOTE EYLANDT

A lot of people from all over the place, all the half-caste people were sent to Groote Eylandt [the CMS established this school for half-caste children in 1921]. Groote Eylandt was a wild place. There were no Aboriginal people in the mission, just only half-caste people. Well, we had no choice. There were some older ones there and some like Fred Blitner and Gerry Blitner, and Harry Hamilton and Harry Huddleston. There was a big mob. They were big grown ups after and they are all over the place, some still alive, some dead. They married different people; white men or their colour.

Anyhow, I stayed at Roper until Reverend Warren came. He was a minister and I went with him to Groote Eylandt on the boat called *Holly*. It had a crew of four or six Aboriginal people, they got flour or tea for pay. There were no vehicles at that time. There was a T-model Ford, but it was broken down. I walked up there to the mission, all covered in this sickness, whooping cough. They put me in a dormitory with the other kids. But I couldn't mix up with those other people, because I had whooping cough and about three different kind of disease, sicknesses you know.

There used to be a big pineapple plantation there, and one log cabin was right in the middle of all that and they put me in there for three months. They fed me through a little pigeon hole. I couldn't walk around. For three solid months I was there. After a while I come all right and then I was let out.

Around about another six months time another big mob come up, about twelve, thirteen others, same colour as me. They were staying there. Reverend Warren took me down to the Emerald River that comes out in the Gulf of Carpentaria, for being baptised. I was named Harry Camfoo. My first name was Harry but there were just too many Harrys there. He said,

> 'I think I'll change your name and call you Jimmy. Oh, you'll like that name. You're still wearing your father's name.'

'All right.'

So he baptised me there and said, 'From now on you're Jimmy Camfoo.'

*   *   *

Those days, I was starting to grow up then. We all grew up there. And Reverend Warren said, 'Oh well, I think all the mainland mob should go back to their parents now.'

Well, no use following our parents, especially me. I was taught Ngalakan language, but after all that I'd forgotten it.

> **Tribal groups and languages**
>
> A number of languages are spoken in the Roper River area including Nunggubuyu, Ngalakan, Ngandi, Rembarrnga and Mara. Aboriginal people have always spoken several languages from adjacent areas. Today they also speak the local creole (Kriol) and English.
>
> Languages reinforce identity and are seen to belong to particular country. Many names have several versions from the different languages. Tex' identity comes from his 'cultural' (language and ceremony), historical (life experiences) and 'racial' (physical, genealogical) heritage. He speaks a fluent and colourful style of English characteristic of Aboriginal cattle workers as well as Kriol which he refers to as 'pidgin English'.

I'd been there for about three or four years then. By that time I was somewhere around about eleven or twelve years old. And Warren, Reverend Warren, said,

'Oh, we gotta send all them, all the mainland mob back. Go back to see their parents.'

Well by that time we forgot our parents. They was going to get all the Aboriginal people, the Indigenous people, civilised.

They were all wild at that time. They could fight like, whoa spear! Well it was nothing, spearing one another. One time Reverend Warren and one other missionary, they went down to stop them mob, Balamumu people, fighting one another. You know, Balamumu people and Inggurra people. They all fighting people that mob. Pay-back you know.

The Balamumu people come up there early in the morning and they speared one blind old man there. All the others, they tried to help him. They fought but there were too many of them. Some of them ran away, swam across the river right up the mouth of Emerald River. This old fella couldn't move or anything. There must have been a dozen spears right from his body right up to his head. Anyhow, they couldn't do nothing because Reverend Warren took his .303 and so they gave up. They didn't spear him. That was one story that I learnt after we had left Groote Eylandt.

*   *   *

We used to be paid for pulling up that weed. It grows here too. We used to pull them by roots and we get so much, sixpence or sevenpence, fivepence, like that. You pull it out by the roots slowly. If it breaks you might get like a penny or couple of pennies. But if you pull it up, straight up, slowly like that, you'd get sevenpence for it. We made our money that way, and we used to go up to the bit of a shop they had there and buy pocket knives or string or something like that.

I used to go for pocket knives because I used to play around with pocket knives, making spears or woomera [spear thrower]. I was a great one for cutting up tables. Breakfast time, dinner time, we used to go and eat at the table, the boys here and all the girls there. I used to cut the tables. And a fella called Mr Thurman, he was a mechanic, he found out and he took the knife off me for two, three weeks and then give it back to me.

*   *   *

Where we had our dormitory there was a big mango tree with a lot of fruit. One was hanging down, a great big one you know and I used to walk past it. It was all nice and juicy and for maybe a few days I was watching that one. All the bigger boys was watching it too. Well I took that mango, broke it and shared it and it was raw [unripe] but we ate it anyway. The boys said, 'Hello, hello, somebody pinch it.'

Well they went and told the boss he come around.

'Who pinch it? Who pinch it?'

He asked all of us. I sat quiet, and then I owned up. He said, 'You're a bad boy.'

So then they had to chain me up every night. Chain me up with a little dog chain, tied around my leg. For punishment. And in the morning they used to come up and unlock me you know, so I could go and have breakfast and go to school.

Anything there like that they used to punish us that way or we used to have to weed around the fence, you know. The grass or vine or things you know, that grow along the fence. They used to give us hoes.

'Do this for a week. That's your punishment.'

We were weeding and some of the older girls used to come and help us to clean up, pull the grass with the hoes and help cut the grass down, help us that way. Like they were our sisters and our aunties, half-caste girls. When the boss come up they used to run away you know.

Anyhow, some of the girls had been at Groote Eylandt since they were small, they grew up to be big girls. They would get married you know, and later on, one by one or two by two, they came to Roper. They found a boyfriend and got married, and some went to Roper Valley. Some went to Darwin, Katherine, all over. Well Katherine wasn't there yet and Darwin was only just coming up, there was only just some little houses. Some of them still alive. My cousin Marie Bourke, she's still alive. She's getting old now. Others, I can't name some of them, they all over the place. Fred Blitner, he's at Beswick [Station].

Eventually, half the girls from Groote Eylandt come over to Roper then. And one was Connie Bush. She made a life story [autobiography] of herself.

Groote Eylandt went on after we left. They got all the Aboriginal people and gradually teach them, and they learned this and that. They had about two, three hundred people there after that.

Kinship

These children could trace their relationships to each other through marriage, descent or connections to a common relative. The network of kinship extends kin terms to more distant relations and would have been of great importance when these children were separated from their parents and their country.

They were taught to be individualistic and to strive for their own betterment rather than to identify as part of a community. The experience of being taken away could disturb the dense interweaving of kin with its obligations and loyalties, thus undermining a child's cultural identity.

3. ROPER MISSION

Anyhow, they shipped us back to Roper River and in that time there was Mr and Mrs Port. They were missionaries, like a sort of manager, at Groote Eylandt. Well, they transferred him back to Roper and they took us on the *Holly* boat, thirty, a big mob of us.

My mother and my stepfather was at Numbulwar. That used to be a saltpan there then, and Roper River mob used to get salt from there to salt corned beef. They knew we was coming back, and they were waving, waving to us. And we went alongside the bank, just not far away. And we couldn't know them! We all sat looking at them and they looked at us. They didn't know.

'Maybe my son there somewhere? My daughter there somewhere?'

That day my mother knew I was coming there and she got a canoe. Her husband was Juree. Juree was a Mara man from Borroloola, and he ran away with my mother after Power Jack died. When my mother was walking around Roper Bar way they found one another and fell in love and he took her away to Borroloola.

Anyhow this Juree and her and another couple of boys [Aboriginal men] they load their belongings and dugong, cooked dugong, and they paddle all night until they come up at Roper River. I was there then. They come up and saw me. I didn't know my mother. I ran away from her, you know! After a while they talked to me.

'That's your mother, that's your mother! You don't want to run away. That's your proper mother! Old Florida!'

After a while I knew. I met up with my mother. She never used to stay long, you know, just enough to visit me and take me walkabout, eating plum and things like that. Green plums, you know?

Old

The term *old* is used in Aboriginal English as a term of affectionate respect, and denotes maturity rather than age. White people often misunderstand and protest when they are respectfully called *old man* or *augaman* (Kriol for *old woman*), by Aboriginal friends. Unlike the European practice of women marrying slightly older men, traditionally an Aboriginal woman's first husband would usually be considerably older than she is, though later husbands may well be considerably younger.

The missionaries used to look after us, you know, feed us. But they treated us rough [brutally]. It's a long story, it'll take over a month to tell you the history of what I've seen. You see I'm leaving all the stories behind too.

In our school days at Roper they never used to teach us much. I learned to read and write and do bit of alphabet and things like that but not like the kids are doing today. If I'd have been taught like the way they doing now, I wouldn't be here now. I would've been somewhere sitting at a desk or something, you know, doing big jobs. But I never had education. I can only just barely read and write.

But what I learnt is how to work.

Like after school, two hours before knock-off [the end of the working day] we used to pull a big three ton wagon up. About two miles we would pull this wagon. Girls on one side and boys on one side and two of the biggest man on the shaft. We used to drag that up, up the side of the hill, and the woodchoppers would have the wood all stacked up there for us. We loaded that up and take it to the cooking place for children's tucker. Saturdays they used to cook in the kitchen, but not an inside kitchen, just on an open fire.

It was really, I tell you what, it was pretty rough. Our school teacher wasn't a first-class teacher like, just our own colour. No-one from down south or proper full-class trained teacher. They never sent a full-class teacher to teach us. It was just only our own colour.

Well back at Groote Eylandt we had a school teacher there called Miss Cross. She was a middle aged lady and she used to teach us. When we were sent back to Roper we had only one woman. We had Connie. She was not bad but we didn't learn properly.

*   *   *

At Roper, when I was a young boy we used to swim across the river. That old mission river was infested. A lot of maneaters, crocodiles in there, saltwater ones. But we used to swim across that river. On the other side we'd go and look for food. That was straight after morning school, like dinner break time. We'd get together and swim across the river.

'Hey it might be just about school time now!'

And we used to swim back just in time.

Every night there's two or three crocodiles there. Three, four dogs were taken by crocodiles. I don't know how we used to miss. We never used to fear. I used to be the last one. They reckon they always take the last one. Maybe they'd had enough!

I nearly got taken there once.

I was a good hunter in my young days, in my childhood days. I made a little spear of mine. Every time I'd get any little break I used to run down to the river for fish. Well, this time I went and I seen some rifle fish under a freshwater mangrove. They were still, no movements. Luckily it was low tide and there was little bit of an island. I jumped to that island, to a clump of pandanus alongside that river bank.

I was wanting those rifle fish to come near me, so I could spear them. I was just going to throw it and something told me to look back. I looked back and there's a big crocodile just there behind me. But luckily I was up, I was about this high, about six feet. I was in the middle of the pandanus there waiting for these fish, to spear these fish. This crocodile, he was ready to pounce on me! I looked back, I tell you fair dinkum, I jumped from there to right over that island and straight up the bank. I went straight up the bank and I looked across, and he was still there.

That was a woman's swimming place. That's where they used to go and bogey [bathe] there and go off for school. The boy's swimming place was a couple of hundred yards down. I wonder what would've happened if the girls would've run down and dived in. As far as I know, right through the times that we been kids, none were taken, although very near though. A lot of woman used to go down and get water too. Luckily these woman never got taken, because he was underneath the tree root and the root was about big as my arm and he had his nose right underneath it.

We used to carry lot of rocks and ant bed [termite mound] and things like that and throw the rocks into the water to frighten the crocodiles away. Once they threw rocks and they waited and nothing happened, so this woman she reach her hand down and got a bucket of water and the crocodile couldn't jump up because he was underneath the root of a tree. But he opened his hand out like that and he just scratched the woman's arm like that. It wasn't bad; she didn't even went to hospital. She was lucky.

4. TREACLE

Oh, this is a funny part. A boat called *Noosa* used to bring up the tucker, supplies from Thursday Island. In the olden days time we had the kerosene tin, big and square, filled with treacle. It was a bit darker colour than golden syrup. Well, they had a big store there, about that high off the ground. They put all the flour, tea, sugar all stacked up in the corner. We used to crawl underneath.

'Where that treacle mob stacked up?'

'Here they are.'

We'd get a little nail, punch a hole in where there's a crack in the board. Make a little hole. One bloke lay down like that, he got his mouth open for that treacle to drip in. Another bloke watching.

'Hey one bloke coming along!'

Sit quiet. It didn't worry the boy laying there, because he can't see anything. But he's got his mouth open. We used to come out, oh, sick as anything, go straight for the water, gut all full of treacle. After we were finished we would get a piece of rag or a little stick and clog it up. Lots of boys watching would make out like we're playing.

Everybody got to know. They come with a little tins like that and little coolamon [wooden dish] and fill it up and plant it in the bush somewhere and night time we can start into it.

'Next one! Next one! Next one! Next one!'

One tin gone. Well, all that stuff was there. One tin of treacle there, another one on top, maybe six in a row or twelve in a row. And all the bottom part, there was no treacle. When the missionary opened the first one,

'Eh, it's empty!'

'What's wrong?'

'There's a hole.'

But we used to let some of it run out, make it look like it had a hole before and then we had to leave some on the ground. And we would rub our track out. Anyhow, nothing there, all the bottom part, was all completely empty. Finished the whole lot, all the bottom part and get a longer wire then, enough to put a nail in. A lot of funny things we did. Couldn't help it if you were hungry.

*   *   *

Especially Silas Roberts, he would grab anything, and feed himself through there. And he used to get .22 bullets and chuck them in the fire. We'd hear the bang, hear the noise there. One didn't go off and he went to strike a match ... phew! It clipped him. Just lucky it never got his hand. He run out, he looked like someone else. He burned his neck here. He looked up and they could see the blood.

'I don't know what's that, but the .22 bullet creased in there.'

He was lucky that day. We was only kids then.

5. BUSH TUCKER

My mother could get over a thousand, maybe a thousand different bush tuckers. Out in the bush you know. A lot of the white people don't know and even some of the Aboriginal people, they didn't try it. At Alice Springs and Adelaide and all through that area, even at Queensland, Aboriginal people they don't know what we eat here.

> **Bush tucker**
>
> 'Bush tucker' is now the name for the food Aboriginal people collected and ate before white people arrived. The stations and missions began to supply dry rations (flour, tea, sugar) and in the 1940s rationing was made general. Mainoru supplied dry rations for the 'walkabout' period, but people still relied on bush tucker. Besides game, many kinds of plant foods are used, but with today's closer sedentary life these are not readily available.

Everybody knows goanna, everybody eat it. Turkey, emu and kangaroo, like that. But like berries and things, people don't know. A lot of berries here are poison. You'd eat them and start off feeling sick and after while you might pass away. There's different lot of yams [edible root] too that are poison. Some of them all right. They might make you sick for a couple of days but then you come all right again.

Honey and even the bee eggs are good too. You crush them up all together you know and oh, it's beautiful. There's brown sugarbag—you got about three or four different kinds of sugarbag [honey].

There's one where the bee flies in, in the hole, it's like a funnel. Well that's a different kind. And there's another one, you just can't see the bee. It just goes straight into the hole. But this one with the funnel is about a foot long. You can see it and see the bee come out of it. And you can cut it down. Honey comes first and then the yellow stuff, and then the eggs. It's marvellous to see how they work. Sometimes we used to get a feather and catch the little bee and stick a little feather on it. You can't see the bee. You see the feather, white feather. You see it goes up to that tree and you see him land, right where the door is,

'Oh, there's one!'

Something like that. Even the ground sugarbag. We call it just 'ground sugarbag'. They have their ant bed or dry tree, right on the ground, a sort of waxy entrance where they go in. The dog used to find it for us. We trained dogs to smell sugarbag.

We made that bomb to blow up fish. It's written in Lockwood's book [see Douglas Lockwood, *I, the Aboriginal,* 1962]. If I could read that book again I'd remember.

Anyhow, this billabong, well it doesn't happen now, but those days, they used to cut a hollow tree and throw it in the middle of the billabong and when the jabiru pelican comes around and the crane, the fish used to race to that hollow log, to get away from them. And it has a little sort of cut to put a stick with a little fork through the little hole to pull the log out.

Then they walked in, it was waist deep. They walked around that billabong, hunt all the fish into that log. It might be, oh, for half an hour, you do it quick. You get a big mob of grass, dry grass and stuffed the two ends up, so the fish won't run out. The log was about, maybe six feet. They stuffed up two ends up so they won't swim out. Stuck this little fork in through that hole and pull it up to the bank then and open that up, and oh, fish about that high! All sorts of fish!

* * *

There's a lot of bush medicine. I think the white people they know some bush medicine now. Like little berries and leaves that you got to boil for fever and bits of gum, from gum tree. Then you boil that and wash it down and it makes you feel good inside, it goes into you. The green ants is good for headaches and good for tooth or fever and things like that. Plums, green plums and billygoat plum is good for asthma, but I think the white people know about that.

If you have a belly-ache, or guts-ache or you can't toilet, you eat the yellow part from the sugarbag. We call it the egg but it's not the egg. The yellow part, you mix it up with water and then you drink that. It works like Epsom salts. Things like that.

At Roper, in the morning we'd pack up and go, out bush. As long as I got flour and tea and sugar. Well, I never used to go for tea and sugar, but a special bit of damper, johnny-cake, something like that, they used to keep me going that way. Anyhow, we went up to that place there and I got a very terrible sickness.

'Oh, they been do it to him, blackfella way.'

I was on my last breath. For four solid days I had some sort of fever that can kill anybody. They tried to do anything, trying to cure me.

They cooked, they boiled all sorts of fish for me. Now that was in my dying hours, I was just about dead. They made me drink half a coolamon of fish soup and that was a good medicine. In the morning I got up fresh as a rose, running around, playing with the boys. I always think about that. That's why when I have something, fever or cold I always go down and get a catfish or a sleeping cod or barramundi or any of them, got to be fish though, boil that up and let it cool off and then drink it. Oh, beautiful, beautiful.

> **Sorcery**
>
> Tex refers to the 'blackfella way' of making someone ill by sorcery. Because white people show little respect for such forms of knowledge, they are usually kept secret (A.P. Elkin, *Aboriginal Men of High Degree*, 1997).

6. RUNNING AWAY

And one time I thought to myself, 'I think I'll leave the Roper and start roaming around.' I said to my friend Roger, 'Let's run away from mission.'

But we didn't run away far. We went in to the next station at Urapunga. Well the bloke was called Earl there, Mr Earl. Alma was there, she was only young girl then, Alma Gibb. She mightn't know that now [she might have forgotten]. And old Stingray, and Lizzie she was there. Anyhow we run away to Urapunga. We only stayed there for three nights. We said, 'Oh we go to Saint Vidgeon more better.' That was me, Phillip Roberts and Roger.

'You know what we'll do?'

'No.'

'We'll walk back again and then pinch a canoe and paddle across the river, tie the canoe up, then we'll walk to Saint Vidgeon. We'll go there.'

There was a lot of people there too, like the old countrymen you know. Father, uncles, sisters and aunties and all that. But we never got that far. We went to old mission and we spent that night in there and they found out that we were there. So they got us. We got a good hiding for that.

*   *   *

Next time I run away I remember, old Jack Marney was there. He was a copper there. Jack Marney. Mr Port wrote a letter and said to me, 'You take this letter up to the policeman at Roper Bar.' I didn't know why, but that was the report that he made about me when I run away!

Well Bill Huddleston, he was about a year or two older than me, anyhow, they was going to go muster that morning. They got the horses in the paddock and everything ready to go in the morning. I said to him, 'Hey mate, how about you give me one of them horses?' So I can go up to Roper Bar. It was a long way for my age, 'cause I was young hefty little bloke then.

'Yeah, well all right. Don't you say anything, eh?'

'No. I won't say anything.'

So I got a string, like Indian style. And I found a good mare too, by the name of Midget. A good handling mare she was. Got up early in the morning and put a sort of a noose around her neck and took the hobble off and jumped on bareback.

Away I went!

Early in the morning. The day after, Bill's father said,

'Oh, one horse missing.'

'He come out through that gate there. That gate been open.'

'Oh, doesn't matter. Leave it. Doesn't matter.'

Well I got to come out through that gate, that Wolmudja gate. I got to come out there. And then I went to Ngudjelaii, Wadgelai. We used to call it Ngudjelaii, white man used to call it Wadgelai. Big billabong, about couple of miles away from old mission. Away I went. I had bit of tucker. I went to the Wilton Crossing and I run into a few blokes there. One bloke called Bun. And Tithanboi Thomson. He's still alive, Thomson. He got that place at Nungalary, at Roper. He was a young boy then, same age as me. He was up for same thing too and the copper told him, 'You better get back to the Roper mission!'

He run away with me that time too. Now it was my turn for going in, but I didn't know I was taking a summons letter. He said, 'Hey, mate! You give me that horse and I'll ride it back to Roper.'

'Yeah, all right then, I'll walk from here.'

It wasn't far, about five miles, from Wilton Crossing to Roper Bar. Got a new police station there. Anyhow, I told him, 'When you get back to Ngudjelaii …'

You see when we used to muster horses we took the hobble off from one side and put the hobble on the outside so you can walk. So I said, 'When you get back there, throw the rope, that little halter thing, throw it away and put the hobble strap around the mare's leg. Never mind which way, left hand or right hand. Put one, and throw the other strap away. Look like she broke a strap.'

'Yeah, I'll do that.'

I don't know what he did, I never asked him. I went on, I walked there and I crossed to Roper Bar. On the left hand side there's lot of cane grass. I fell asleep there and when I got up I seen a big yellow cat looking at me. I didn't know what to do. Then after that I walked up to Jack Marney.

'Oh yeah, I knew you were coming!'

'Here's a letter,' I said.

'Oh, you run away eh? Oh well, come on, in that cell.'

Cell's still standing there. I know that cell. Anyhow, he took me in there, locked me up. Never gave me water, nothing. There was a lot of bags of wheat there, for chook's feed you know. And one pawpaw there, just one pawpaw. I ate that. I was starting getting into the wheat, eating that wheat, that chook tucker. I was hungry and they never gave me any supper! In the morning, I thought now he'll want to give me a hiding. Open the door and said, 'You little bastard!'

He knew my father was Jimmy Camfoo. He knew me too.

'Ah, how old are you?'

'I'm nineteen.'

But I was only about fourteen.

'Ah, don't tell me bullshit. What you run away for?'

'Oh, that missionary no good. Been too cheeky [rude]. I want to go and look for my mother!'

'No, you're too young. You only about fourteen or fifteen. You're not eighteen.'

'Yeah, I ...'

'No, don't talk so much!'

Well, anyhow. 'I'll give you a good breakfast, I'll take you home in the car. And if you run away again boy, I'll take you into Darwin so everybody can laugh at you!'

He sat me down, gave me a good feed. And the police tracker was called Nipper. He called me *bunji*. I called him *bunji* too, blackfella way. He said, 'Oh *bunji* what you mob been doing?'

'I been runaway.'

Bunji

Bunji refers to a relationship of friendly intimacy, founded in the kinship system where it formally refers to 'wife's brother' who is a particular kind of 'cousin'. Often a man's wife's brother is likely to be married to his real or his classificatory sister so the term is a reciprocal one. *Bunji* is sometimes used nowadays to assert a friendly relationship with a whitefella.

I had good breakfast then. Milk and rice and sugar and tea, piece of bread.

'Oh, you can come back with me.'

So me, Nipper, him and his wife, went to Saint Vidgeon to see old Jimmy Gibb, but he wasn't there.

'He's got to go that Borroloola road, up past Saint Vidgeon. He went out mustering. He's going to be home in three weeks time.'

So they took me down to Roper, on that side of the river, down the old mission. They took me up there.

'So there he is! I told him not to run away or I'm taking him to Darwin.'

I said, 'Sorry, sorry for running away', to that mongrel bloody missionary.

'Oh well, go and join in the boys again.'

*   *   *

So, I was back there. We always did a lot of things, and we always used to get caught. We couldn't help it, because we were hungry. Getting up late at night and going in the garden, melon patch and take melons and things. They always say, everyone,

'Who's been pinching melons?'

'It's gotta be Jimmy! It's gotta be Jimmy!'

Sometimes I used to take blame for other people's problems. Oh, I was a real outlaw then, they reckon. After a while I grew up to be a nice boy.

7. THE BIG FLOOD

That was old Mission, that year [1940] when that big flood come up, and all the flat country was under, and only the hills was showing. It rained for two weeks, non-stop. All that flat country was all under water. So, we had to go to this place called Monoganni, might be a couple of miles away.

'You get all the half-caste peoples to come. Go on this boat *Holly*.'

This *Holly*, the boat, it was at the mission that time, at Roper, with our supplies. They didn't have a chance to unload all the food, the flour and things like that.

Some had to swim from tree to tree, going to Monoganni. There was snakes and goannas and centipedes, you name it, all up in those trees.

There was some people went on board the *Holly*, but us mob, we paddled across to that hill called Munoga. Rain like that, oh, goodness what a terrible nightmare that was. We had to get spinifex to build a bit of a shelter, but rain went through it. Every morning we had no house. In the morning we used to see the *Holly* there in the middle of the water. The skipper Harry Hamilton, he said, 'We might have to shift from here and go back to a calmer place, where there's not much current.'

They was going to go. But one day we got up and it was missing!

'Hey, where did *Holly* go? The boat?'

What happened was, the boat was tied on a poinciana tree with big chains. But then the poinciana tree was gone. The current was too strong and rooted up the poinciana tree. They floated down. It was a dark night too.

Well they didn't know where the river [Roper River] was because the river was over its banks! Just alongside the big river, there was a tree with its branch broken and the branch was pointing straight where the *Holly* got to come in. It come side on. Bore a big hole in it. Everybody then calling,

'Come on! Look out! There's water pouring in!'

They all run up the tree. Every time the lightning strike they saw that big tree. There were two women. One was pregnant and had a little baby. Connie Bush was there and three crew and one Mr Perryman. One was a mechanic and couldn't swim. Mr Taylor we used to call him, we didn't know his first name. We used to call all the white men *mister*.

Anyway, they all climbed up that tree. I don't know how the boat come undone from the branch that made a hole in it, that it was stuck on. It rolled down the river anyhow. Every time that lightning strike, they could see another tree, alongside them, not far from where they were up that tree. The water was coming up, coming up. The Aboriginal people were sitting in water on that tree. I don't know how that tree never washed away. This fellow Mr Perryman, he can't swim. Then the daylight came and we were standing up on that hill, you know, watching for that boat.

'Where the boat went?'

And then somebody seen three figures swimming. They swim down the river. Of course the current was strong and they were going from tree to tree. I said, 'Where, where boat?'

'Oh, finished. Drowned.'

All of the people were there, hanging up in the tree!

We had a little boat there, we named him *Heath*. It picked them up, and brought them back. I don't know how they never got washed away but everything was okay. That *Holly* was the boat that used to take us to Groote Eylandt and back again, then go up to Thursday Island and pick up our rations. And no-one got washed away. No-one got killed or anything.

The boat was laying about a couple of hundred yards from the river bank. When flood went down, there it was. All the flour and petrol drums and things from the house. And chickens, goats, roosters, they were perching on top of the trees. Some got washed away, poor things. All the tucker, all the flour got floated away and washed into the hill where we were. Water come right up over the bank and leave the petrol drums and even flour. We used to walk around after and pick up flour and make a damper, somewhere in the scrub there.

After a while people used to go up and tell the missionaries, 'Oh, they got flour!' We used to get punished for that, for stealing I suppose. Missionaries!

*   *   *

This was not where Monoganni, Ngukurr is now, but the old mission. It was a starving place, not much tucker, but a good lot of friends—Roger, and Kevin-boy and Gilbert. We used to make little bows and arrow and little spear. We lived on birds and ducks. We got on all right.

We were cut off for about three or four months then. Anyhow, they put on the pedal wireless and rang up Darwin, and all that and a battleship come out to save us, to bring tucker for us, food and everything. I don't know why they sent a battleship. It had machine guns and everything. They come up the river, and after a while the old people got together and had a meeting.

Well everything was all down, no water, dried up, country was dry, everything was destroyed, buildings, everything. So then we decided to build a mission at where she stands now, at Ngukurr.

When we got up to Ngukurr, that's the time we got married. All the young boys started to get married then, because the girls were running around single and the young boys like us was running around and we got married. I worked there and I come to be a really fully sized stockman.

The missionaries had cattle and horses. And then I was sent over to the mission. I used to muster and I come to be head stockman there at the mission.

8. THAT WAS THE COPPER!

At Roper Bar in those days we never used to get rations, even the old pensioners. We'd move away from there and have bush tucker for a week or a couple of weeks, and then come back again.

Where the Roper Bar is now, well where the old mission station was on the other side of the creek, the police station used to be there. They had little rooms and a lockup in one corner.

Well one time we were going to shift and go to Hodgson Down Crossing, Yanda Yanda Billabong. Anyhow the old people had their talk together, to move out and have bush tucker for a while. Well that night, I suppose, dad said to mum, 'Go up to this policeman in there and ask him, you know, for a tin of tobacco.'

She goes up there and she comes home with flour and sugar and tea and tobacco, as a payment you know. That was the copper [how the policeman behaved]!

A lot of them police were single too you know. And there were not many cars on the roads those days. It's hard if you've got to go back to Sydney to get a woman. It's a long way. There was no plane. It was the quickest way. It was a matter of wasting a bit of money to get bit of flour and tea and sugar and tobacco.

Those police, they made us touchy too, you know. Every time Aboriginal people'd see a white man they used to dash into cane grass, down the

---

Sexual liaisons and the law

Liaisons between white men and black women were forbidden by the churches, and disapproved by society generally as well as being illegal. Many (although not all) white men saw such activities as shameful or exploitative.

For Aboriginal people they meant something quite different. These exchanges were often intended to establish and secure ongoing relationships of reciprocity [see Ann McGrath, *Born in the cattle*, 1987]. Aboriginal men claim a moral virtue in not showing jealousy in relation to their wives' sexual activities [see Tex' story Chapter 15, page 53].

Government officials could not stop the sexual exploitation of Aboriginal women on stations, as the infrequent visits of officials were known in advance. But the surveillance of police and patrol officers did reinforce the sense of shame and illegitimacy attached to relationships between people from different racial categories. It also made it more difficult for white men who lived with Aboriginal women to formalise their relationship and take responsibility for their children.

river! There's a lot of cane grasses there that grows on the side of the bank. They were frightened of the policeman, and used to go away somewhere. But night time, that's a different matter. That's when we manage to get our good tucker. Even meat, things like that the policeman gave them. That's why I always say that policeman was my stepfather.

Roper was the main place, base sort of place. Anyway we used to go back there. Or, go to other country. There's a lot of places we used to go where there'd be tucker. They gave us tea and flour, sugar and tobacco for same thing. Maybe, tomahawk or material, something like that you know. Then go on to another place. After one week or two weeks, come back again. They had to take tobacco out, because they started smoking. Same thing happened like that. It was like that for years. After a while after I was grown up, I used to tell those stories to other people.

The women loved it. But they couldn't help it you know. They got to do it. The oldfellas say, 'Well you gotta do it. You gone with him up until now. No, you got to do it.' And that's how most of we half-caste people were born. Marie Bourke. She was one of them that's been kidnapped and taken to Darwin.

There's no shame. Even my cousin, he's got a father, the policeman who took over Roper Bar. It was like a routine job you know. She'd go up a couple of weeks and then come back again. Go up for another week there, same thing happened.

Anyhow, those old people that died now, I used to love those old people. When I was growing up, when I was full grown man I used to talk to the Aboriginal people. They used to tell me lot about these sort of things. I'm talking out of experience of being with them, here and there. Old people used to tell me all these sort of things. Those days was hard for us sometimes.

9. MISSIONARIES

Those missionaries, a lot of them, they were not too good. At Roper they were all right but they used to go muck around [have sexual relations] with Aboriginal women there, Aboriginal girls, living up there at Ngukurr. There's a couple of kids walking around under their name. Nobody said nothing about them but everybody knew. Nobody squealed on them you know. They just kept it quiet.

When a European used to muck around with dark girls, before the Citizen Right [the usual term for the rights gained in the 1967 referendum] come up, they used to get caught and they'd go in gaol or get fined you know. Or get moved out of that place. Native Affairs used to go around people that worked on the stations, and check up on all those things.

This missionary, Stanley Port. I reckon if he was alive today I would've gone and punched him straight in the bloody nose. And his wife was more worse. And they're supposed to be missionaries you know! CMS stands for 'Church Missionary Society' and they used to run the place, like they were the boss. They used to live in Sydney.

Well some missionaries was really good, you know. Some of them was really bad, really cruel. I was a great one for them. They used to belt me around. One time we come over and she [Mrs Port] said to somebody, I think it was Margaret Hall—she was one of our teacher too and she was a half-caste woman—she said, 'Let all the children come out early. They going to go and get some yabbies for me.'

Well, Roper River's a big river. But that was down the old Mission. And they gave us bit of meat, little bit of fresh meat to go and get these yabbies for her. They gave us an hour and I couldn't get any!

I went up. We all line up and she comes around with the basin or dish or something, and we had to drop the little crayfish in there. I was the one that never got any. I tried my best to get one but I never got it. And you know what the flaming mongrel done? She had a black bitch called Pompy. Oh, a cheeky thing. She come out with that. 'You didn't get any, eh? I suppose you been sleeping!'

Well she got Pompy alongside there, near all these big logs you know. Got the Aboriginal people to watch to see nothing happen to her, only to me. She grab me by the arm like that and make out she's giving me a hiding and then let the dog bite me! Yeah it bit me, and I still carry the mark here somewhere. Here, look! You can see it. It grabbed me and tore my shirt. That's for not getting the crayfish!

Another time, my mate got caught with a bow and arrow. We used to make our own bow and arrow for shooting birds for our tucker, because we never used to get much. And she said, 'Stand over there! Take your whatsaname.'

We used to wear a sort of a thing like a petticoat, but a frock, you know, like a naga [cloth] with a knot here or a sheet tied. No underwear. Well, 'Take that off! Throw it out!' He was naked. And you know Mrs Port she said to him, 'Stand over there and don't look back!'

She got that bow and arrow.

'I'm going to shoot you now!'

And poor thing he was shivering and crying. She never let the arrow go, but frightened him.

*   *   *

Another time, I was the one who copped it!

We used to help, work in the garden and we had a couple of rows of tomatoes right alongside the road where the missionary came out and go to the church every morning. One tomato was starting to get ripe. I'm the one used to water the garden and watch that tomato when it's going to be ripe. It was starting to get ripe, it was getting that yellow colour. I took it! And they found it. I think Mr Port must've knew that I took it.

Anyhow we used to go, girls line up one end like that, from the biggest girl right down to the smallest you know, and the biggest boy right down to the smallest. Then we'd sing out grace and then go and grab our lunch. A bit of food, nothing much. Anyhow Mr Port said, 'I gonna smell that ripe tomato. I'm gonna smell it.'

But he knew I was the man. He was smelling, sniffing and he went around, right down and I whispered, 'He's smellin' his own arse!'

Well he walked past and said, 'Who said that? Who said?'

Nobody said nothing. They didn't let me down. And that yarn went through there, spreading like wildfire, right up to the old station, 'He's smellin' his own arse!' I'll never forget that.

If we used to do wrong, they used to have us stand on the fence post. No clothes, in the blazing sun for half an hour. And there was this big blackfella there with a whip, every time we fall off the post because it's too hot you know. For half an hour, or fifteen minutes, he'd chase them up the post again. He was called Morrdiki, a Ngalakan man. He had a big 'tom-tom', a leather, like a cleaver thing with a little handle, but it's a strap. He used to whip us with that to make us climb on the post.

It wasn't him really. That's orders from the Christian people. He used to whip us if we do anything wrong, steal anything or something like that. And when we'd fall over, or sometimes we'd get crook or maybe we jump off, he'd come up with the 'tom-tom'. He was sitting there, sitting there, poor bugger. Girls too. Girls on one side, naked. We never used to have any underwear, those days. Fancy young girls sitting up there on the post, naked!

*   *   *

> ### Racial Language
>
> Many words that have been part of normal language for years and remain part of the local vernacular, have been outlawed in the public domain because they were used to express contempt or to entrench racial inequality. *Coloured* or *part coloured*, *half-caste* and *yellafella* were commonly used terms in the past which are seldom used now except in remote places such as Bulman. *Boy* referred to 'full blood' Aboriginal men who worked for white men. *Boy* was used to differentiate them from both the white workers and the *myalls* or 'wild bush blackfellas' who lived apart from whites. *Gin* and *lubra* used to be the Territory vernacular for an Aboriginal woman and Tex uses them in this original sense.

There was not enough tucker you know. We used to go in the goat yard and get some milk, with the girls. We had five, six hundred goats, so we used to get some milk that way.

Down Sydney the church used to go round for donations, collecting money to keep us going for food. And all the good foods that used to come up, the missionaries ate it! Not us mob, not the people that were living in the mission! They used to eat it, themselves!

They used to put all the empty cans and things like that in a big sack-bag, and then they would send all the big man to go out with the boat and throw it in the middle of the river so that all the top-knots from Sydney that think they was looking after us, so they won't find out about it. But that was the dirty work they done.

We had no bed, only blankets on a dirt floor made of ant bed, no mattress, no pillow. The school teacher used to come and count the blankets and if one was missing they'd get worried.

We used to prise the window open. They'd flog you in the morning if you stayed in camp with our parents all night. Sometimes, if they were in a good humour on Saturday they might let us go to the camp to our parents and come back Sunday. At school holidays the teacher used to take us coloured people out for two weeks camping in the bush. We were not supposed to mix, Aborigine and half-caste, but we were mixed up all the time. Separate sleeping and holidays, but we played games, Aborigine and half-caste.

10. GIRLFRIENDS

We had girlfriends. After we really grew up, we had girlfriends. Like it's just natural you know. After we grew up they taught us what it says in the bible: 'thou shalt not commit adultery'. We'd go and have bit of a sing-song you know, choruses and things. Then we'd go back and they would lock us up in the dormitory. Sometimes we'd go down and see our parents, our mothers, and come back late and we had to sleep outside then. After a while somebody squealed about that and they would leave the door open or just shut it. Then they never used to lock us up then for a while.

They had dormitories, girls' dormitory and boys' dormitory. We couldn't go near the girls' one. They'd lock us up, but we couldn't go without it because we were old enough, we could feel it then. We used to get in somehow, into the dormitory. We used to find a way to get in. The windows were way up but we would kneel down with our hands and knees, and somebody climb up the back and jump in over the window that way. When we got to the girls dormitory, the girls'd say, 'How many boys there are?'

'Oh so and so, and so and so.'

So all of their girlfriends would come out. Over the window. So we got there. After a while the missionary said, 'Oh, we gonna lock them up this time, lock the windows.'

So somebody had an idea.

> 'Hey look, how about we dig a hole underneath, in the house and out the other side?'

Well the girls helped with that too you know, and we used to cover it, cover it up with iron, just ordinary iron. Oh, they never really knew about it for long time. Well we said to the girls, 'You mob stay there and the men, the boys will come up to you.' All the young ones, we'd wait till all the youngsters there were asleep. Three or four of us would go underneath and come back up the other side. Tie up our feet with a bag so that they can't see our track, away we'd go. Then we go, scratch, scratch on the door. 'Oh they're there.'

So they used to open the hole, crawl underneath and come out inside! Get up about piccaninny daylight [dawn]. Out. Off. Back. They found out after when one or two of the women are pregnant. That's how they found out, oh then they knew! Oh, hiding! Oh, they give the boys hiding, I tell you they did!

After a while then everything was all right, you know, after a few missionaries had come around there and we heard what God said. When He put that big flood and destroyed everybody, all the people, God said, 'Go back and multiply and get all the people back again.'

The missionaries didn't know we knew that too, you know. They say it's against the law, but it's only the missionaries that made that law. When they found out about all the girls, they had night watchers walking around all the night but we used to get around that. They expected that we weren't real smart.

After a while good missionaries came up, and they never used to bother us. When you grow up there, nineteen, eighteen years old, we were old enough, but we'd be still in the dormitory because they didn't like us going down the camp, especially the half-caste. They wouldn't allow us to go down there.

Missionaries tried to get some of the school girls to marry. That was hard too because well, some of those school girls that were pregnant, although they had sweetheart, they had promise husbands too. Their promise husbands were waiting. They'd been in schools and after they grew up they had to go to their promise husbands. A few was married in the church but not officially because he wasn't a registered parson. That marriage, it wasn't legal we found out after.

But they were hypocrites those missionaries, as far as I'm concerned. Some of them were really really Christian people. But some of them was just mongrels. A lot of them just kept running around under the missionary name, pretending to be good. They mucked about with the girls themselves. They used to say, 'Thou shalt not do this!' or 'Thou shalt not take the neighbour's wife!'

They taught us things like that. But after a while they forgot about that and become heathen I reckon! The missionaries that had been there all of the time, we helped them too, you know. Because we used to go and get a woman for them. Some of us used to help them to get one. I know a couple of them. They asked us after a while. Maybe I shouldn't talk about them, because it might make

> **Promises**
>
> A promise husband or wife refers to marriage arrangements which involved many relations. A young girl was promised as the future wife to an older man who was then responsible for looking after her, known as 'growing her up', until she reached the age of marriage. When missionaries and government officials began to object and interfere with these arrangements, Aboriginal people saw the girls as having lost their protection and proper care from a senior man.

them a bad name, but they knew at that time what they done wrong. Well, they just resign, went back to Sydney. They had to resign.

It's not like today. Because everyone didn't know the law and we never used to go up and complain. The old people didn't worry about it. We was all just young people, we didn't care what goes on. Native Affairs those days used to come out and find out what was going on. But Native Affairs didn't do anything.

1. LEAVING ARNHEM LAND, FINDING MAINORU

I was born at Mainoru, then we went back to Malyanganuk and back again [mid 1930s]. My father was working there. I was the eldest I was, like little Annie's size, [six years old] and Willie was the second one. No Dolly or Ronnie yet, only me and Willie walking, and Smiler and Dorothy were in the coolamon [wooden dish]. Smiler was born at Malyanganuk. Well, we walked all the way from Malyanganuk, sleeping by the road for three days all the way to Annie Creek. Stopped there for three days and looked around for all the bush tucker. We had a rest, we had naked foot, you know, bare feet.

Only my father and mother and *gokgok* [grandmother], my family, were there. The first time we saw white people, Willie was frightened. Only me, I wasn't frightened.

All right. We came up from Annie Creek, we slept at Dingo yard across the Wilton River and came up to Bulman waterhole and slept there one week. From there we walked on the top road to Emu Mountain, through Lindsay and to Horse Creek then next day to Mainoru.

We found Mrs Farrer, old Judy there, married to old Billy Farrar. That old man, old Billy Farrar, he was a really wild white man. Judy Farrar was my Aunty, full Rembarrnga. She was at Murrawangi before. They used to run the old Arafura station, they call that Murrawangi. It was opened by Billy Farrar. We followed them to Mainoru. Old Billy Farrer was a stockman at Mainoru first.

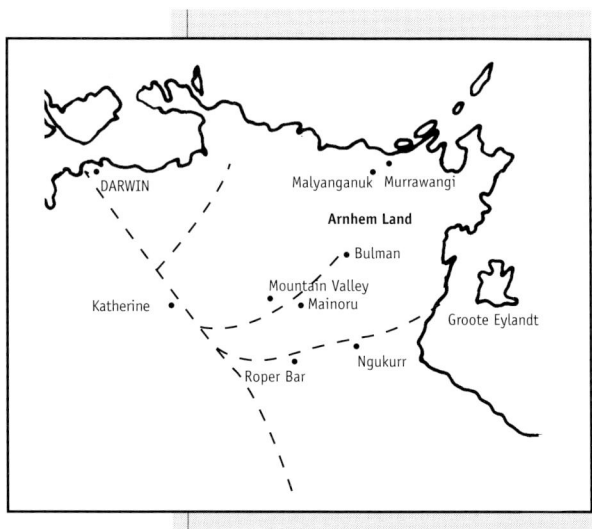

Frontier violence

The managers of early stations in the Arnhem Land area are said to have tried to shoot all the Aboriginal people. At the same time, the spearing of cattle and indeed of white men is also often recalled by Aborigines.

But despite their violent acts, white men such as Billy Farrar and George Conway were accepted as part of the social world of Aborigines. Farrar was married to a Rembarrnga woman, Judy, and left her £46 in his will. George Conway also had a long term Aboriginal woman companion.

Young women at Mainoru (early 1950s)
From back: Nelly Camfoo, Dina, Rosie, Dolly, Dorothy, Abie, Janet, Pixie

Me, I was interested in Mainoru straight away, even though I reckoned white people were cooked. Their skin look like boiled meat, and I was sorry. I reckon my uncle Billy Farrar was cooked. But then I said to myself, 'This person's not cooked. I see he's got two eye, one mouth, a lot of tooth. He's a human being!'

Before we had kangaroo, porcupine, snake. But then cattle were all around, buffalo were all around, donkey and horses were all around in the bush. We didn't kill bullocks, only buffalo for eating.

We were sitting down [living] there at Mainoru, and Jack McKay came from somewhere. He was asking if he could take over that place from Billy Farrar. The boys [Aboriginal stockmen] were all working then. Jack McKay stayed at Mainoru and Billy Farrer was at Mountain Valley then.

I was a little one yet. Everybody was working, whole lot. Florry, Lucy, old Chuckaduck. My father worked. Although he was myall and he did not savvy [understand] English properly, but he could savvy a little bit of English. He always worked.

Me, I liked work. We had nanny goats at Mainoru, 500 goats. I was goat shepherd girl. I used to go with old Lucy. My aunty, old Judy Farrar, used to make me work in the garden, planting the garden, and she used to tell me to go and milk the goats. If I didn't do what she told me, bang! She gave me a hiding to make me have sense, good sense. She had a whip, a stock whip, and she was belting me in the back. I used to do everything and that's why I came good I reckon. My teachers were my father and mother and aunty.

We were sitting down there, and the biggest mob of *mununga* [whitefellas] came up to Mainoru. After Jack McKay came, his mother came, then his brother and his sister, Mrs Dodd. They used to have us all there. There used to be three or four hundred Aboriginal people. They liked blackfellas that McKay family. Pity we lost that girl Heather Dodd. She'd be still running that place. We wanted her to get married but she didn't want to be married.

11. HORSES

So after a while I grew up. When I was somewhere around about eighteen, nineteen, I left school and I wanted to be a stockman. This friend of mine that died, he had a brother Wilton. Wilton's brother, Bill Huddleston, me and him we grew up together. He died now, poor thing.

> **Names**
>
> Although Tex is reluctant to speak the name of a dead person, he is conscious of whitefellas' confusion and will name people, sometimes in a roundabout way. The taboo on speaking the names of deceased people is lifted after a long period.

I used to go with him riding horses. Every time he went mustering, I wanted to go too. 'Hey, I come with you?' He would go and tell his father, Walker.

'I can take Jimmy Camfoo too?'

'Yeah, you two can go.'

We were friends.

One day they told him to go and get this bangtail [cut tail] mare. She used to pull wagon to cart wood. We went round and found her. There was a little chestnut horse called Charlie. We used to feed him and he would come around like one of the pets. We broke him and that's the horse I rode. We found them both, got on and they took off. Billy was in the lead, me behind, going flat out. All of a sudden the horse wanted to go that way, I wanted the horse to go this way. So I fell off and my leg got caught in the stirrup and he dragged me from here to that little hut there. Billy looked back, he said 'Oh!'

Charlie pulled around—he was just a quiet little horse—and just stood there. I was scratched from head to right down. Luckily he took me under a tree. Billy said, 'You wait here, I'll get them horses.' He went round, and I was sitting under a shady tree. He come back with the horses and we went home.

> 'Ah, Tex, got dragged by a horse. It's finished him. He won't ride a horse now for couple of months, that's a punishment for him.'

Then another time, me and Roger. Roger Rogers, Gunbukbuk, my best friend, we were together all the time, we never parted me and Roger Rogers.

Gunbukbuk was his blackfella name. He's still alive. He's got a place, somewhere down the Roper there, I forget the name of that country.

'We'll go riding.'

We were supposed to look after the horses, me and Phillip Roberts. He was same age as me too. We said to Roger, 'Hey, how about we go walkabout with you?'

We had three horses, one each, but no saddle, just bareback! We went around taking kangaroos. Just where Ngukurr is now, we were at 'Old Missionhead', we used to call it. We run into a kangaroo there, at the river. So we chased him and my horse hit Roger's horse and knocked him over and broke Roger's pelvis bone. Phillip said, 'Hey, look out! Now we'll be in trouble.'

Well we didn't know what's wrong. He's yelling out, you know, with the pain. He's crying like anything. Phillip spoke, he said to me, 'I have to go back and look for help.'

They were worried then.

'Ah, what happen now?'

'You've got to go there, pick him up. He's got a broken bone.'

We weren't far from the river. Roger was crying for water, and there's no water. I ran down and filled my mouth with water and came back and poured it into his mouth. We were waiting till they came up, then we carried him down and put him on a dinghy called *Taemar*. Richard Hall and Dan Daniel come up, so me and Phillip went back with two horses that we had. We rode back.

Naming

Aborigines had to understand and use two rival naming systems.

Whites gave European names to Aboriginal people and places. Officials would use these names only, thereby denying the Aboriginal names and creating their own cultural landscape.

Aboriginal people were also given nicknames by white men in accordance with the outback tradition of naming people by their physical characteristics. Men such as Hitler, Smiler and Bandicoot would have been initially unaware of the meaning of their names to other whites.

Nelly's brother Smiler Martin with Ben (circa 1959)

Photo: Courtesy of the Museum and Art Gallery of the Northern Territory

There were no doctors at that time. Mr and Mrs Port were in charge then. They rang up and the flying doctor from Cloncurry heard it, Dr Fenton. So he come up and got Roger and took him up to Darwin. He was there over a year, he come back a big man. I was a big man too when he come back.

*   *   *

I always wanted to be a ringer, but they said, 'Oh, stockman no good.'

Me and Bill Huddleston we worked together to be carpenters. I worked three years in carpentry with a bloke called Richard Hall, at Roper. But I always wanted to go back as a ringer. As I grew up, by that time I had no promised wife. I was just, you know, free. I did actually have sweethearts but that was on the old Mission. When I grew up to be man I was married to Ruth then, at Ngukurr. Ruth was the first woman I had. I left her and all the kids and she was pregnant for Tim, the last boy of mine.

Tex Camfoo as a young man (mid 1950s)

2. HARD WORK

I was a cook for the stock camps before World War Two. Riding and camping and cooking, from five o'clock in the morning to eight o'clock at night. That's the sort of woman I am. I had a really hard boss, and a really strong boss too. No work, no tucker, get sacked. If I'm working and get chucked off from horse, my boss used to tell me, get on again, jump on the horse again. Well that's the only way you can train people. That's why I'm a hard woman now. But I think I've had enough hard work. I want to get relaxed.

My mother and father had training blackfella way from my great-grandfather and great-grandmother and grandfather. I was trained blackfella way from my mother and father and aunty and all those relations. Good people, work all day. My aunty trained me to get bush tucker and to cook my own food and look after myself, and when I came to whitefella, I am like that now. I can live your way or our way, out bush.

At Mainoru we usually worked from five o'clock in the morning until eight o'clock at night because it was a cattle station. Me and Florry and Lucy, we all were olden times ringer. My Aunty Judy was really the best ringer. She was throwing bullocks, roping and tying bullocks, drafting, earmarking, branding. We never saw any money. When the McKay family was in town, we used to get three pounds or four pounds. But before they used to call money seven shillings and sixpence, then it came to be 75 cents. Well that's how we used to get it.

Nelly Camfoo (right) and Glen Stuart (circa 1960)

Photo: Courtesy of the Museum and Art Gallery of the Northern Territory

Those old people used to get rations, a little bit of sugar and flour. We were working for clothes, we were working for tea and sugar. Before the war there was no money. After World War Two everybody got money. Black people, and white too maybe. I don't know about white people.

It took me a long time to learn English. But then I was beginning to pick up English properly. It's a pity I didn't go to school, but in my day there wasn't any school and I was married to this old man, Tex. Anyway, I've got a pencil and paper in my brain. Mrs Dodd's school, that's nearly this time [recent]. I might still go to night school and learn A-B-C-D and all that. I can write my name.

> **Language**
>
> Nelly can speak several languages including Kriol, which now has the status of a separate language, one historically composed of English words amalgamated with grammatical features of the local languages. It is commonly spoken by most Aborigines and some whites of the cattle country. Nelly spoke to me in English with elements of Kriol terms and grammatical constructions.

12. NUMBER TWO WAR

When that number two war broke out and when the Japanese were starting to bomb Darwin, we were at Ngukurr then. They were starting to bomb Darwin and a mob of lighthorse army was at Batchelor. They come with a mob of horses, through Beswick, through Jalboi, right down to Roper to Roper Bar. They made a big camp there. Dick Harris was missionary there then and they said to him, 'Oh, this army gonna come and make a post at Monoganni. And some of the boys from here has got to join up with them.'

There was me, Bill Huddleston, Des Harrison and Sam Thompson. There was four of us taken. So we joined up with them. Then there was a couple of big army trucks took us down there and we made a camp. There was one place called Kangaroo Island, we used to go there for a week or two weeks. Then we come back and another mob go. Like, for watching the river so no submarine or anything comes up the Roper River. Then after that we made another post at Green Island, that's further down again. From there down to Mount Joshua. That's the time when this midget submarine went to blow Sydney Harbour up. Those days they didn't have the proper machines to pick them up, but they used to hear that engine going, of the little midget submarine.

Anyhow I worked for them for a while there. I never got any money out of them yet! We were working for army, carrying water for them. My best friend, he was Des Harrison. We worked for them, or with them, for about nearly a year and a half. Maybe little bit more.

*   *   *

There was one bloke there from Rose River, from Numbulwar. A horse threw this boy and broke his leg. But there were no roads—it was just wild, wild country. In rain time, we walked across to Saint Vidgeon with three white man soldiers and a fella called Brown Harrison. We walked right across, carrying him. It took us only one day to Saint Vidgeon Station, and we tried to make a bit of a strip so a plane can land and pick him up. But it wasn't good enough so we had to carry him down to the old mission. There was a landing there. Anyhow, we had three or four horses there at home and we made a stretcher for him, and we got bogged down, right down to our knees, over our knees. It was raining like cats and dogs. I said to this Corporal Humphrey, I said, 'Ah, why don't we put him on a horse?'

He had splints you know right up his leg. So we put him on a horse and we led the horse for a while and he said, 'Oh, the pain, pain, pain!'

So I had to get him off and lay him on the stretcher again. We carried him. We got there when it was just piccaninny daylight. That little boat used to carry troops up the river and down the river and shift army here and there. It had a little machine gun on top of the cabin. They waited for us there. We put him on and took him up to Roper Bar. The army truck took him to Katherine, then up to Darwin.

Then they took us over the river. Before they went up to Katherine we were on this side of the river and they took us across the river again, where we camped. In those days I was healthy and really strong. Me and Des Harrison we used to jog along right up the river to Ngukurr, that's about seven, eight miles, and stay there for about five, or ten, twenty minutes, then run back again.

We were with the twenty-three platoon and they wanted us to go to New Guinea from there. And me and Bill Huddleston, we wanted to go and join the army and go with them. Probably I would have been the first one to get shot. A few years back, after the war was finished, we found out, a lot of the boys got killed. Some of them was alive though.

Des Harrison, when he got over there he was a bomb aimer, and then after the war he come to be a major. After the war, he got a place breeding quarter-horse. When I worked here, he come up all the way from south to see me. Him and his wife. His son was already working here, young Des Harrison. They come up, I went up and met him at Top Yard. Took a barra' [barramundi] there and cooked it and brought him up here. He was good old bloke. After he seen me here, they went down to Ngukurr to see Sam Thompson mob that was working there at Monoganni.

Anyhow, I left Roper, that was in the number two war, and I hitchhiked from Urapunga. I was going to go to Mataranka, following my mother. But apparently she wasn't there. It was all full of army. So I worked. Then these two army blokes that took me, they said, 'No use you coming into camp, to Mataranka, it's all full of army.'

So I said, 'I might as well stay here at Elsey.'

3. WAR

We stopped there at Mainoru. I was eighteen now, or seventeen, and World War Two came and we went to work for the army. One lady, white woman, she was getting us for washing up dishes and cleaning the house, for housework. We worked at Larrimah, Mataranka, Tennant Creek. We came back and then the army heard that war was coming near. The Japanese were fighting the army. The army took us to one big settlement at Tennant Creek. They bombed Darwin when we were at that place called Donkey Creek. Everybody was going to work. No matter what language, they took them up there to the big big settlement run by Welfare. Native Affairs it was in those days. We had to work, work, work! Thirty or forty young girls were working on that army job. Cooking, washing, ironing clothes. Some died but some are still alive at Barunga. We always wanted to help fight the Japanese.

Japanese settled down [stopped fighting] from the war then. Everybody was breaking out and coming back to their own country again. But I still worked in Darwin. I liked to work with those army people, army ladies. Not only me but five other girls were going to Darwin at that time and they bombed Darwin airstrip. That settlement used to be at Berrimah first, before that it was at Bagot. From that time I was sick of it poorfella me, so we went to Katherine and all the way back to Mainoru, to where I was born.

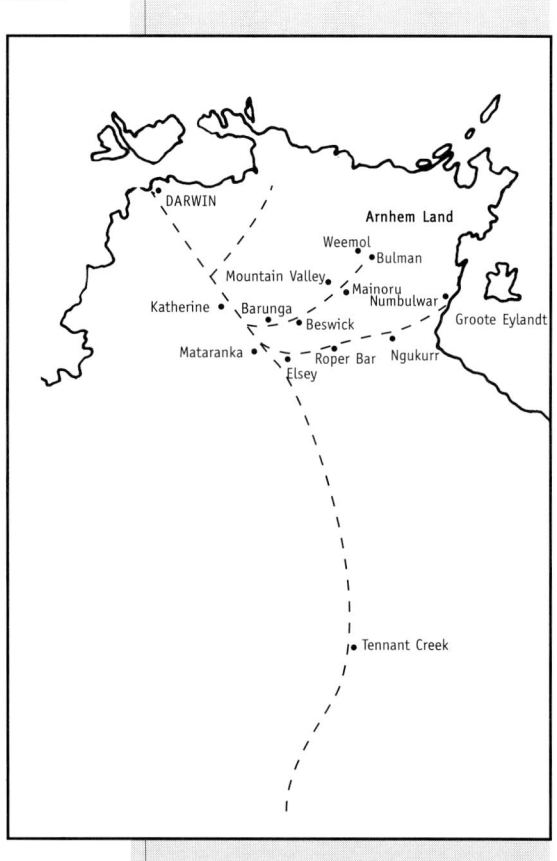

13. ELSEY

Where Jilpinga is, that's where we camped with three or four army trucks. And those two young blokes said, 'We'll run you back to the homestead.'

I didn't know anyone there at Elsey. The old people knew me straight away so they took me down to camp. Some of them, they all died now; there was uncle and stepfather and my aunty and my mother, they knew me. I was camped there for three or four days and this oldfella that I call Paddy, he went up to the homestead.

'Hey, one yellafella's down there.'

'Who?'

'Fair dinkum, he come up from Roper, with that army truck.'

'What his name?'

'Oh, his name Jimmy, Jimmy Camfoo.'

'What? Jimmy Camfoo? Oh, I think I know that fella. Well I don't know him but I know his father. Old Jimmy Camfoo. Oh, go and get him and send him up!'

Old Harold Giles was his name, that whitefella that was the manager. And anyhow, Paddy come and say to me, 'Hey, boss want you go up.'

So I went up.

'Ah, I think I know you. What your name?'

'My name Jimmy Camfoo.'

'Oh, I know your father old Jimmy, I know him, we used to be together all the time. Why didn't you come straight up here?'

'Well', I said, 'I didn't know anyone!'

'Course I was shy, and didn't know anything and that was the first time I had gone anywhere like that. Anyhow, he said, 'Go and see Hong.' That was the cook there, Chinaman. So I went there and he says, 'The boss told me to give you breakfast!'

So they gave me breakfast, started to talk, you know.

'Oh, you Chinaman too are you?'

'Yeah, I'm a Chinaman.'

'Who your father?'

'Jimmy Camfoo.'

'Ah. I know some of these Camfoos.'

Anyhow I started work. Then Harry Giles come up and seen me again, 'How'd you like to be my batman?'

Well, I didn't know what to do. I couldn't. But I said, 'Well okay then.'

I started to work for him, private boy, you know. Like, me and him used to go into Mataranka, pick up stores and things like that. I started going good at ten bob a week. And then I helped the carpenter. Me and him built one house. Me and him used to have a row every day.

Then I come to know Jack Powell. Danny Farrar was the head stockman. That's Billy Farrar's son I'm talking about. Then me and a young bloke Joey, yellafella, started to put an electric wire to catch brumbies. After we'd finished that we used to go round and see if it's all right.

You've got this little box and you run the current through. There's one copper wire from tree to tree. You follow that one round you know, and if a leaf touches it or a branch fell, we had to run back and switch the box. But sometimes we used to be cunning and get a rag and tie it round and fix it up that way. But sometimes you just don't do it properly, and you get BANG, big shock.

*   *   *

We used to do that work, and then Harry Giles, he said to me, 'We got some stuff to take to Roper Bar.' So me and three or four old people, away we went. We had to take a big generator.

Well about twelve miles this side of Hodgson Downs, that was an outstation for Elsey, we got bogged. Well not really properly bogged. We could've come out but this oldfella didn't know that there's about four gears. That's one first, second, third and top. Four gears and a reverse. Old Chev', it was an army truck. Well I used to drive Chevs before and I keep watching this oldfella how he changed that gear, you know. He said to me, 'You better watch me. You might be able to drive this later on, you know. I'm getting too old to drive trucks. You're a youngfella.'

I was plenty jealous too. He was quiet oldfella, talking quiet. Anyhow he's going there, 'Oh, we'll have to start walking.'

We were about seven miles from Hodgson Downs. We got a big pole and put a big rope round the generator. Anyhow, two blokes, one bloke got the front and another one carried the back. We walked from here, like from the station, about two kilometres. Then we had a spell and I said to him, 'You know what? That vehicle got about four gears: first, second, third and top!'

I said, 'Let's go back and try.'

So we went back.

'See that's top: first, second, top gear.'

'All right, we try.'

We couldn't get it going. The battery went flat. We'd had couple of flat tyres before we got stuck there and I'd just seen how they used that jack. You got one big piece and you got another little piece that's sort of like a crank handle. So I thought I could make it work to crank the engine. They call it the 'dog' where you put a crank handle in, and the two pins goes like that and you crank it. But this one's a jack, it's got four squares. I looked at those four corners. 'I wonder if I can file that and get those two corners into the place?'

And I said, 'Have you got a file?'

'Yeah I got a file.'

A three quarter file, a little one.

'Give me a hold of that. I'll try and file these two corners.'

I file that one so I can get that dog to fit in there and grip around the two little crack where the two pin goes. Anyhow, it took me just about two hours. Eventually I got in and I tried it, and it took a hold. I said, 'Get on the seat now and switch the key on.'

One go! 'We are on our way now!'

I said, 'Put it on first gear.' It just crawled out! Away we went.

14. GEORGE CONWAY

Anyhow we had to come back to a place where they hanged that Chinaman there one time, called Mole Hill. We had to cart some rail for a yard there because it got burned. We went and trapped brumbies there.

Old George Conway was contract mustering for Elsey then. George knew my father and I wanted to work for him. He'd come in to get rations. He told me a story from somewhere around east Arnhem Land. They were chasing the blackfellas on horses and there was an island not far away, maybe a half a mile. The only way they could escape was to swim to the island. They got to the island and they were all right. But then one blackfella ran out and danced around saying 'Oh we got you mob'. But they had these long range rifles and I don't know if it was George but one of them shot at him and got him too. Killed him [see Douglas Lockwood, *Up the Track*, 1964].

> **George Conway**
>
> George Conway took part in a government sponsored attempt to rid the area of Aborigines in 1909. But Conway was also a companion of Aboriginal people, especially Rooney, who he lived with for many years.

George Conway, he was a rough old fella. They named the road after him, because he was going to build a station there when he was contracting for Ted Collins at Beswick. Just before you go up the jump-up [escarpment] there, that house on the left, they call that Conway.

When I got a job there at Beswick, I don't know how I got that job. It was a miracle. There weren't many people there then. There was Ted Collins and his wife, a Philippine girl and Teddy Liddle from Alice Springs. And Walker, he died, and Jim Barella he died and Paddy Banana, well he died too. And two old ladies. I forget their name now. They used to be goat shepherds, look after the goats.

Ted Collins, Cowboy Collins they used to call him, was working with George Conway. I worked there at Beswick taking in cleanskins [unbranded cattle]. I was a really good worker, so he said to me, 'You want to work here for me, I'll give you good money, I'll give you good wages.'

I was only getting ten bob a week from George Conway. Collins said, 'Well I'll bump you up to two pounds a week.'

So I worked for two pounds a week. Oh, talk about hard work! You get up about six o'clock, till about seven o'clock in the afternoon we used to knock off work. Talk about work! Anyhow after a while, he said, 'How about you become head stockman?'

There was only about four of us, five of us. Wilton Huddleston, they picked him up too, from Katherine. They said, 'Hey we got tons of work, how about you come and work?'

'Oh yeah, old Tex there, eh? Oh well, Jimmy there? I'll come then.'

Anyhow, we worked there at Beswick. And that *Leshia*, that big boat from Thursday Island, used to carry rations up to Ngukurr and then up to Urapunga and then Roper Bar. Beswick used to get their rations from Thursday Island too. Well we used to jump on that *Leshia* with Ted Collins and he used to take us down to Roper Bar and then used to let me and Matt Thompson off there for maybe one week or two weeks' holiday.

When I was at Beswick, Yellow Bob used to come up there with old Jack McKay. There was wagons those days. Yellow Bob! I don't know where he was born. They reckon he's from Queensland, some reckon from Roper Valley. He could talk Ngalakan better than me. I can't talk Ngalakan at all, but he was more whiter than me! But Larry and Dick got him the same skin [tribal subsection] as them. Anyhow, he had leprosy. He was a ceremony man [took part in ceremonial life] too. Jack had him there for long time on Mainoru. But apparently he had to be sent to quarantine island, you know that island for leprosy, and he died there. But he was Ngalakan too. He had a daughter Alice Roberts, Phillip's sister. Eric Roberts was her son. I don't know where Yellow Bob come from but he could talk Ngalakan with Larry and Dick, and Florry and Lucy and Rosie all them, you know brothers and sisters, same skin as us.

*   *   *

Before I was taken away to Groote Eylandt when I was eight my name was Harry. But at Groote Eylandt I was called Jimmy.

Anyway, I was thinking about Tex Morton, the singer, and I thought to myself, that's a good name. There was a parson at Ngukurr called Harris and I said to him, I want to be baptised.'

'Okay then. What name do you want.'

'Tex James Camfoo.'

'I'll take you down there.' We had a reservoir there alongside the river and that's where it happened. He baptised me Tex.

I changed my name into Tex but I still wear my father's name, Camfoo. James Camfoo. When I was baptised I thought if I change my name I'd become a Christian, but I didn't.

*   *   *

Then Ted Collins sold Beswick to Native Affairs. George Conway started his station there for a bit, but they kicked him out from there when Native Affairs bought Beswick. He couldn't carry on. He was getting too old, so he sold all his horses and saddles and packs and hobbles and all things like that. He sold it to Native Affairs at Beswick. The mob of goats was still there on that big hill, running around in the last two, three years. People used to come out from Beswick and shoot them, and eventually they finish them off now.

I worked for Native Affairs [Native Affairs Branch of the Commonwealth Department of the Interior] for a while at Beswick and then me and the head stockman had an argument. I had a plant of horses [enough horses and equipment needed for a droving or mustering project] of my own now, at that time. About twenty-nine horses I had. I bought them off Ted Middleton, five pound a head because I was cramped [short of] for horses. The bloke called Gilbert Blitner, me and him travelled down, all the way from Beswick to Roper. Then I ran the camp there at Roper.

After two or three years then I went to Urapunga. I can't give you the exact date and year but it was about 1952 when I was at Urapunga, and about 1954 when I left.

> **Beswick Station**
>
> Beswick Station was bought by the government in 1947 so that the Native Affairs Branch of the Commonwealth Department of the Interior (later the Commonwealth Department of Territories) could train Aboriginal stockmen. It operated as a government cattle station with the Aboriginal community which congregated there as its labour force. The staff were government employees. New housing and rationing policies were trialed on this property.

*   *   *

Fred Olsen was a pom. He used to pilot Eddy Connolan's aeroplane that come every fortnight with the mail. We bumped into each other at Urapunga and he said, 'How about you run a camp for me?'

I said, 'I know this country inside out. Well, okay, I'll take the job.'

So I used go mustering through all that area, then go back to Roper and look around up there, then joint muster with Ngukurr stock camp around Harkup area. That's where a Chinaman man died, on the Urapunga boundary. He had stones built up there for a fireplace and paperbark and all that. He came up all the way from Murrawangi and he had a place down at Bigetti. Aboriginal people chased him out of there and he followed the Wilton River down and thought 'I'll stay here at Harkup'. And you can see the same thing there, stone stove and fireplace, a bit of a *gundi* [hut]. Then he died and was buried there. His name was Harkup, but he's still got an Aboriginal name. And later, that's where I used to meet the Urapunga people for joint muster when I was on Mainoru.

Then I got sick of it. I spent nearly two years there at Urapunga and the money wasn't much good, you know, so I thought, 'Oh, well, I'll go back to Katherine.'

15. MAINORU, MURDERS AND MEMORIES

Before, when I was working at Beswick, when Ted Collins was there, Jack McKay would come up. He was owner at Mainoru. I said to him one time, 'How about me coming out there to Mainoru and do some carpentry?'

I learnt to be a carpenter for three years but I didn't like that job. I wanted to ride horses and things like that. And Jack said to me, 'Oh, I got big mob of men in the camp.'

So I didn't worry about it then.

But when I left Roper with the same pilot, Fred Olsen, the plane was, oh, really rough. You know, rocking and rolling and things like that. I was terribly sick when we was landing at Mainoru airstrip. I was sick in the bag, that brown bag, two of those bags that was full of whatsaname. And Jack McKay came up, and Nelly. Well Nelly was there and she was married to Larry. Anyhow, when I got off, there was Jack McKay and old Jimmy Dodd, his brother-in-law and Nelly and two or three others, old girls, Florry and Lucy, Rosie and Fanny, those sisters. Oh goodness, I was sweating, and anyhow I said to Jack, 'When you going into Katherine again?'

'Oh, next week.'

And so I said, 'Well, could you take me in when you go in? Could I stay and come with you to Katherine because I'm terribly sick?'

'No worries, stay.'

So I stayed there. After a while I used to get around with Jack and we would come back up here, to Bulman. All there was here was the mining.

> **Mainoru**
>
> Jack McKay bought into Mainoru Station in the 1940s. His old mother, his brother Sandy, and his sister Margaret joined him there in the 1950s with Margaret's husband Jimmy Dodd and their daughter Heather.
>
> The McKays had a very positive approach towards the Aboriginal community, though a racial hierarchy was also apparent in the physical separation of the homestead on the hill from the 'the camp' where the Aboriginal community lived. But unlike many pastoralists, Jack McKay was not hostile and did not oppose the ceremonial life. He assisted Aborigines to travel during the wet season to conduct ceremonies, so that Tex and others could continue to fulfil their ceremonial obligations.

Jack McKay (1950)

Stockwork. Jack McKay and Tex Camfoo
(circa 1955)

It was about a fortnight before he went into Katherine. So in the meantime I started to do odds and ends and things like fixing up fences and chopping some timber for posts and things like that. In about a week's time, well I knew Chuckaduck and old Dick and Larry and Florry, and Lucy and Nelly. Some of the old people were there, and they said to Jack, 'We savvy that yellafella, our countryman you know, and him good stockman too!'

So anyhow, me and Chuckaduck and Jack McKay went out to get some posts and when he went back he said to me, 'How about taking a job here?'

Well that suited me fine because I wanted to come to Mainoru all the time and that was the only way. There was little money those days, you got about ten bob a week. That was in pounds then, not dollars. I worked there for a year, then on to two years, then he decided to put me on for good.

Old Jimmy Gibb was there too. He used to own Urapunga, but he sold it and came up to Mainoru. He was the head stockman and he took lot of bullocks from Murrawangi to Mataranka. When they come up they said, 'Oh, Jack got old Tex here.'

Jimmy knew me because I had worked for him. And he said, 'Yeah, I work up here regularly. How about you work here with me?'

Jimmy Gibb was a white bloke and he married Alma Gibb after. They had to get permission to marry. I used to go out mustering with old Jimmy Gibb and big mob of boys, Chuckaduck, old Diver and Slippery and all them old people. Some of them died now. They were marvellous stockmen too. Anyhow after Jimmy Gibb was too old and that half-caste bloke Billy Moore left Mainoru because he had Mountain Valley then, Jack come up to me and said, 'How about you take the stock camp?'

'Okay, give me a go for three weeks, or six weeks, and see how I go.'

Well I had been running camps all over the place and it just fitted nicely. So I kept on going at Mainoru for nearly twenty-five years as head stockman. I'd take the camp out and go back. Do bit of overseer's job and doing fences all around, doing saddling work and things like that. I was just like one of Jack McKay's family, they treated as equal, but I never got paid till about, maybe three years after. I said, 'Look, I'm doing all sorts of jobs here.' So they brought me up to twenty-five pounds. I kept on going and they gave me a house and I was treated like one of the family.

My house was near the boss' house. They build a house there for old Jack McKay. He said, 'I don't want that house. Give it to Tex!'

European and Aboriginal law

According to white law, Tex could not be both 'European' and 'blackfella' because like everyone else he was either subject to the provisions of the Aboriginal Ordinance or he was not. This made life rather difficult to say the least, because, for instance, non-Aborigines were forbidden to enter Aboriginal camps without permission from the Director of Native Affairs. Thus Tex was subject to two forms of law and social practice which intersected in personal life in many complex ways.

Ceremonies

Ceremonial life is central to Aboriginal people's law, art and politics and the *Yabuduruwa* ceremony was where Tex' identity and place in Aboriginal society was affirmed. A *Djungaii* is the senior person with major responsibility for the knowledge and ceremonial observance of a particular clan or lineage.

Ceremonial performances verify claims and rights in specific places. Most whitefellas do not know of the existence of this body of knowledge, a fact which makes communication between white and black difficult. Many Aboriginal people are reluctant to expose secret and sacred matters to those who do not respect them.

And at that time, I was starting to go with Nelly. I used to go and take her when my brother Larry was away, then hand her back again. Nelly would come with me or meet me down the river. But after a while Larry found out and said, 'No, I can't be jealous of my brother.'

He used to send over Alice to get tobacco. That's the way it was. Then Larry said to Nelly, 'He's my proper brother ceremony way. If you want that man, have it.'

Through these years I was waiting, four or five years. I used to go and visit all my brothers. But I wouldn't stay down the camp because I was both ways. I was European and I was blackfella.

There wasn't any Aboriginal places like we have now. It was just only bush country. There were a lot of old people from Milingimbi, Ramingining, Maningrida, and all these outstations all over the place. There wasn't any Land Rights Act, it didn't come in then. But they used to travel backwards and forwards, and old Larry and Dick used to come down Roper to see me and join in the ceremony, like *Yabuduruwa* and all that.

Jack McKay didn't mind.

Anyhow, I kept on going and 'Tiga', Heather Dodd, was only a little girl, about this high.

*   *   *

We used to work about three months in the mustering season.

It was nice and cool, cool weather. I used to muster from right around through Arnhem Land. Old Jack would say, 'Don't go out!' Or he'd say, 'Go out, I want about three hundred bullocks to sell. I'm getting short of money.'

So I'd go out, say for about three months, get a couple hundred bullocks and muster them into a bullock paddock at Mainoru. Maybe two hundred or three hundred bullocks. I used to ring up Darwin then, and buyers would come out and see if they want them. They'd pick out the bullocks that they wanted. Then everyone would be buying them.

'Yeah, I'll take him, I'll buy him. When you be leaving?'

'Oh, about five days time.'

It took about eight days to take the bullocks in to Mataranka, and about eight stockmen to a team.

I did all that. We'd go there and sell them and come back again with all the boys. Sometimes I used to take a couple of boys in to take the horses back and another mob would jump on the truck. 'Righto, now all the bullocks are sold, we got some money, now we should rest the horses.'

> **Climate**
>
> Although Aborigines recognise more complex seasonal changes, the Northern Territory has three rather than four seasons, 'the dry', 'the build-up' and 'the wet'. On cattle stations mustering occurred during the dry season, and work around the homestead was done during the wet season.

So I'd take all the working boys and their wives and kids up to Bulman waterhole and leave them for maybe three weeks or four weeks. I used to go and pick them up just before the rain starts. We'd come back and start mustering the horses again, and start shoeing again ready for the next season muster.

Sometimes we'd do an early muster just before the first storms. We'd get some calves, mustered from outside and take the cleanskins in, put the bullocks in the bullock paddock, and the barren cows, fat cows for sale. Then we'd start mustering the breeders paddock at Mainoru. We used to call it 'the bronco paddock'. We'd muster about five or six hundred breeders with their calves, lots of calves. Sometimes it would take us all day to brand calves.

When the heavy rain come up we used to finish again. Then round about April, April or May we start again, start mustering. Oh, that was good old days. We used to go and muster on the boundary with Ray and Neville, the Hood brothers, from Mountain Valley. We used to go in Blackfella Yard and muster through there right along the boundary, right up the top yard, down to Jalboi, maybe couple of weeks. Then we go straight up with all the cleanskins, get all our branded cattle with TOH brand and bring them back to the homestead.

*   *   *

Billy Farrar started Mainoru, him and Tom Boddington. They argue, argue and eventually Boddington left. Before he left he poisoned the salt with arsenic. A lot of people got sick. Don't know if anyone died, but old Slippery got a bit and his foot crumpled up. He could still walk but he was limping. Nelly got a bit of it. Billy Farrar he had the biggest one, his toes got cramped up but he still used to walk around and ride horses. They followed Tom Boddington. George Conway followed him with a big .45 revolver on his hip. He wanted to get square with him. I don't know what happened after that but he went to court.

When I come up to Mainoru old Chuckaduck said, 'I'll show you something.' We went to the paddock about four miles from Mainoru. He said, 'When Billy Farrar was at Mainoru he went out riding around. This blackfella walking into Mainoru found him on the road at a place called Red Lily, and walked up and asked Farrar for a smoke. Billy Farrar got a revolver and shot him straight between his eyes. We put a big rock there.'

That rock was still there. It probably wasn't a paddock yet, maybe he was just riding around, looking for cattle. But Billy Farrar got on good with the Aboriginal people. He did good there because he sold a lot of horses, he put up a trap yard at Puppydog down here and caught over a thousand head of brumbies. He sold piebalds, greys, blues, reds, browns, he sold many horses over in Queensland and South Australia, a lot of good horses.

*   *   *

I always think they should have left Aboriginal people alone like the old days. Maybe ten bob a week we used to get. They were the good old days. Ten bob a week or even a stick of tobacco, tea, jam. These people knew who they were. They knew they were Aboriginal people and they had the whole of Arnhem Land to live on and do what they like. They had two or three wives and things like that. Then they wanted to be citizens, and eventually they got it. It was really good to be an Aborigine and live in the old days.

> **Payment**
>
> At this time Aboriginal workers were supplied with clothing and dry rations, and some cash. Until 1969 they were paid at a rate much lower than white workers since they were not subject to the pastoral workers' award. Such inequality was taken for granted in the past, but is now seen as having been dishonest.

4. THEY SAVVY OUR LIFE

First time, before Jack McKay and my uncle Billy Moore came up, that was blackfella country. When they came in they knew Aboriginal people had some kind of life and still had ceremony, even though we worked at a cattle station. Every night we played didgeridoo and taught the young little kids how to dance for sacred corroboree and the young boys how to make them young man [initiation].

The McKay family never used to care about that. If we wanted to finish off sacred way out from the station, old Jack used to give us motor car and take us mob down there and leave us. When we finished the corroboree he used to come down and check up and pick us up and take us back to work. Not only in the wet season but cold weather time too. That old Jack McKay really knew about our life. He was the first one who savvy us mob's life, and he understood what we were doing. Aboriginal dancing and all that. Although he came from *mununga* he could savvy how we live.

McKay and Dodd family they were really good. They were really interested in our culture. They came and they didn't touch, and didn't ask us about sacred things. They knew we do our own business, ceremony. And they kept us there at Mainoru, I don't know how many hundred people there. They looked after the sacred sites and they never stopped us having ceremony. We used to have *Murrdain* and bogey [ceremonial wash] in that billabong. They never said 'that's dirty water'. They were really good people. Rain time [wet season] we used to come down to Bamarakola and motor car used to come down and pick us all up. Sometimes we had *Yabuduruwa* right near the house. Of course goanna tail used to be there before. All our body was there before, in the dreaming time.

We are all the same skin, but we have a different meaning of skin, different from you. We were all born with skin, but the tribal skin for us, that's different. It's pretty hard for *mununga* to understand.

The McKay family knew about the delivery of babies, about doctors. Annette was born at Mainoru and the others were born at Katherine. Anyway,

Mrs Dodd's school

Mrs Dodd dedicated considerable time and energy to looking after the health and education of the community. She started a school and ran it for twelve years, teaching many of the Mainoru children how to read and write. Stations were being encouraged to educate Aboriginal children, but few took up the task with Mrs Dodd's enthusiasm. Nelly was too old to attend the school.

Inspector at Mrs Dodd's school (1965)

Stolen children

The practice of taking children fathered by white men away from Aboriginal mothers and communities was common in the Northern Territory. Several children were taken from Mainoru station to live in the 'half-caste homes' (see Barbara Cummings, *Take this Child...*, 1990). Mrs Dodd tried to resist these removals, formally adopting Pixie and relaying messages between other children and their families. Eileen Cummings and her children have been reunited with her Rembarrnga family in recent years. Others remain estranged or their whereabouts unknown, though memories of them are kept alive.

Mrs Dodd was teaching the mob of piccaninnies [children]. She had just about a hundred piccaninnies in that school. Mrs Dodd, she was a really good lady. All the McKay mob they were really good. Then they all died. I think the mother old Mrs McKay was buried at Mainoru. Mother and son buried there, and Tex' old Chinese father too, buried at Mainoru, my husband's father, Jimmie Camfoo. He came down there, all the way from Alice Springs. He was mining at Tennant Creek and he had a store there. Tex was born at Roper and he had only one half-sister. Blackfella calls her half-sister but *mununga* would call her cousin. From Ngukkur, Roper, Tex went to Groote Eylandt.

Some were taken away. Mrs Dodd adopted Pixie. Pixie is a flash one. She is another one that was taken from her home. She's my cousin Florry's baby but she didn't look at Florry like a mother.

Eileen Cummings was old Florry's eldest daughter, living in Darwin. She came to see her mother; she stayed here. Eileen told us that Heather Dodd had nobody to talk to there in Darwin. Eileen told her one time, 'Go up to Bulman and go and see all the people that grew you up.' Heather reckon she is going to come and see us another time. We were going to see old Mrs Dodd's funeral, but we couldn't get an aeroplane to go.

16. JUST ROOSTING MARRIAGE

Well after a while, when Billy Moore was mustering, he used to take out three women. Slippery's wife, old Fanny—she's died now—and old Lucy and Florry, those three. They used to go out, maybe two cooking, or only one, and two tailing cattle. Some of them used to be marvellous ringers too.

Well when Billy Moore finished [died], Jimmy Gibb was a head stockman, and he used to take Alma, they used to live together. I think they married after. She was a good cook. She used to go out with her old boyfriend, old Jimmy, and tail coaches [drove the quiet cattle] for a day or two, while we go out and chase wild ones in to them.

After a while when I took over, I used to take Nelly out, because we were married then. Well we weren't really, just roosting marriage.

When I was at Mainoru I was classed as a European, but I used to go down the camp there amongst my family, and of course Nelly used to walk up you know to see me and all that. When I found her she was only about nine years old. Well when I come up here, I think Nelly must have sung me with *Djarada*, that women's business [love magic]. Anyway I sweated for her for about five or six years. She was only about nine when I saw her first.

When I come up to Mainoru, then we decided to get married. The one that I had before, Ruth, well we did go in the church to marry and went through the marriage ceremony and all that. But he wasn't a registered pastor I found out. We never signed any certificate papers or anything.

Anyhow, I used to go with Nelly for nearly three or four years and then we decided to get married. I had to go through Native Affairs in those days myself. Native Affairs, that patrol officer Ron Ryan [patrol officer in charge of Katherine and the area to the east in the 1950s and 1960s] he didn't know I was going around with Nelly.

Marriages and Laws
Aboriginal marriages were not legitimate to many white people. But Tex and Nelly were 'really married' in the eyes of the Aboriginal community because Larry [Nelly's promise husband] had agreed to relinquish his claim on her. When Tex's racial status changed to European, the government's law said he needed permission to marry Nelly.

Well I was a European but I didn't know I was a European, until when the policeman come up and picked me up to take me back to Roper. Teddy Liddle said I wasn't Aboriginal but European, but he said he'd keep it to himself because I'd get into trouble for mucking around with Aboriginal girls.

*   *   *

There was a copper called Dan Spriggs. When he was at Roper Bar I was at Urapunga and he tried to trap me for going with Aboriginal girls. He put pressure on me there. It was six months in gaol, no option, for that. He still had something against me. This time I was way out here at Marylake mustering. The policeman sent Nelly's brother, Willy Martin, out after me. They said, 'Here's a letter about Tex!'

Well anyway, I got a horse, me and Willy, and left early in the morning. We got to the station about, eight, nine o'clock that night. Jack McKay wasn't there. Ron Ryan was there and a copper named John Gordon. He was going to take me over to Dan Spriggs at Roper. In the morning, he said, 'I'll take you back to Roper.'

'Why?'

Anyhow we started, we camped half way at Dalboy. The next day we got in to Roper Bar, and a bloke called Tommy, he said, 'You better take Tex down there, down to Roper, to the wife and family.'

Heather Dodd, Jack McKay, Tex Camfoo and a policeman (late 1950s)

I stayed there one night, and then I decided to go back to Roper Bar again, me and Phillip Roberts. We were camping down the river there, at Roper Bar, at the old landing. Anyhow they walked down, John Gordon and Ron Ryan, they come down to me with a big book you know.

'Where'd you come from?'

'Dan Spriggs brought me back,' I said.

'You married?'

'Yeah, to Ruth.'

They opened the book then, where all the European married to Aboriginal women were written. They got a big book. My name wasn't there! They said, 'Well, we could arrest you for that you know.'

'Why?'

'You not supposed to marry a lubra.'

'Well we married in a Church, you know. It doesn't say that. Now you get me in big trouble,' I said. 'I didn't know.'

Well I got married by a missionary but it turned out he wasn't a registered parson. We kept on talking.

'As far as Dan Spriggs that took you back, he's gonna get sacked.'

I said, 'Why?'

'Well he shouldn't do that.'

He shouldn't have pulled me out from a job like that.

'Well anyhow, I didn't know I was a European.'

'Your father is a Chinaman. They haven't got that Law. You know like, you follow your father, he's a European', he said. 'Your name Camfoo.'

5. 'YOU CAN'T TAKE THAT GIRL'

One time I was working for that Native Affairs bloke Frazer-Allen at Beswick. I wanted to go back to Mainoru so I took my sister Dorothy and we went to Mainoru, footwalking. Sandy McKay saw me there, and he reckoned 'That young girl's a good sort', and told me to come up to the house to work. Then the policeman and Frazer-Allen came from Beswick looking for me. They found me right there in the house. 'We want you back. The manager wants to take you to Adelaide.'

He liked me. If I'd have gone I'd have to go *mununga* way altogether. I wouldn't know blackfellas today. I'd be wearing high heels, socks and boots, everything. But I didn't want to. They asked Jack McKay and he said, 'You can't take that girl. She's already working. You can't take her off the job.'

Good job too. I had good *binji* [a good feeling]. I was really pleased when he said that. So I told that policeman 'I'm sorry. I can't go back with you.'

And I told that manager Frazer-Allen too.

17. WHITE OR BLACK?

A lot of part-coloured people are Aboriginal straight away, you know, and they were all in the big book. But my name was classed as a European. Ron Ryan brought me an exemption card. He took it off Dan Spriggs who took it away from me before. You used to carry the little card in your pocket. So, when you go in the bar, you just show that, so you can drink. And they got a big board up there in the bar where all the names are of people who got a license to go in the bar to have a drink. Well, anyway Ron Ryan had that exemption card for me. He was going to give it to me when we got to Mataranka. But he never told me that. He said, 'Well tomorrow, old Jack McKay still wants you to go back.'

I said, 'Well that suits me fine because Mainoru's a good place.'

Well not only that, Nelly was there too. I said, 'Yeah, I'll go back. No worries.'

Well I had to take that saddle back to Mainoru. Dan Spriggs had borrowed it so I could sit in the saddle instead of sitting bareback.

'Okay then.'

So, I got on the horse and we chased Dan Spriggs. He'd left just that morning. He was camping at Roper Valley and we caught him up there. And, ah, did Ron Ryan argue! He said, 'You got no right to take him,to take Tex away from Mainoru, because he was working for Jack McKay.'

From Aborigines to wards

In the 1950s, the category 'Aboriginal' was replaced with 'ward'—a term that referred to people in need of government assistance—in an attempt to remove references to race from legislation.

The *Welfare Ordinance (1953)* required that there be a Register of Wards. An attempt was made to make a list of all 'full-bloods' to whom the protective legislation was assumed to apply. It became known as the 'stud' book.

Under the Aboriginal Ordinance, exemption cards had been issued to those people defined as half-caste who were considered sufficiently assimilated. Under the Welfare Ordinance these cards became redundant, but because the list of wards was never properly completed, there was considerable confusion about who the Ordinance applied to.

The exemption legalised Tex' visits to the pub with his work mates at the same time as it criminalised his relationships with his wife and family. Tex accepted the law to some extent, but away from the towns people did not take the law too literally.

Dan Spriggs bolted from there again. So we followed him but then apparently he went straight up to Darwin. One year later he was sacked from the police and he started Hay Springs.

When we went to Mataranka, I was sitting back and Ron Ryan went straight into the bar there. Same old pub. And I'm sitting there and old George Conway was in there. He's the bloke that really taught me how to work cattle. And George Conway seen me.

'Oh, old Tex Camfoo there, eh?'

'Yeah.'

'Can he come and have a drink?'

'Course he can!'

George Conway said, 'Bring Tex in here. I'll buy him a drink.'

So Ron Ryan come over, 'Here's your exemption card! I was going to give it to you! But now everybody should know, you're not an Aborigine you're a European!'

So I grabbed that thing and tore it up and threw it away in the bin! And then I went and had couple of beers and oh, everybody was looking.

Then I went to Katherine and I went straight in the bar there. I wasn't drunk. I never used to drink much. I was young then, somewhere about twenty-six, or twenty-three. And then they asked, 'Do you have an exemption card?'

'No, I'm already European, like I can come in the bar, come and have a drink in the bar.'

'Go look his name up!'

He looked in the book and said, 'Yeah, yeah, you all right.'

Anyhow, I went in there and crossed the name off, you know, because I'm automatically a European. But all the Europeans knew I was a ceremony man also. Even at Mainoru I could sneak around. I could go mustering and all that and I could sneak around and go in the *Yabuduruwa*, that ceremony with Larry and Dick. My brothers were all one, same mother but different fathers [see Mudrooroo, *Us Mob*, 1995].

Anyhow, where I was now? Ron Ryan said, 'I'm sending Tex back. Send a vehicle there for him at Katherine.'

Billy Moore came in to pick Jimmy Gibb up from the hospital, and he picked me up too. I was glad to get back here to Mainoru. Soon as I got there, that day, I was on a horse, out mustering again.

*   *   *

Mainoru was the home for Larry and Dick and Florry and all them. But they used to travel around to Roper Valley back to Maranboy in the early days. None of these other settlements were open yet. There was no problem with ceremony. Somebody would come up and say, 'There's a ceremony there, at Roper Bar.'

They have to wait for a couple of days and they're off. Roper Valley, maybe Maranboy, or Joegarden, Jalboi. They used to travel there, or old Roper mission. Even to Yirrkala. These Ngalakan mob, like Chuckaduck, they never used to travel that way, because different country. But this way's for Ngalakan, Ngandi, Rembarrnga, they are together.

Jack McKay used to go out there mustering sometimes. Not often, you know. Just go out, maybe for three or four days and then go back again. And his sister Mrs Dodd was there and we used to call young Heather Dodd, Tiga. Well not everybody called her that, but that was her nickname.

Well after a while when Native Affairs used to come they said, 'Why don't you people start to build up?'

The kids were starting to born, and kids coming in from bush and everywhere to stay on at Mainoru. Then they decided to try and get a school, so Mrs Dodd put in for it and eventually she got it. She was a professional teacher, Mrs Dodd. And I was one of the family. They used to treat me just like I'm one of them you know. I used to use the same table. Nelly and I lived up the house even when we were sweethearts. Ate with them. They were real lover for Aboriginal people. Nelly didn't go to school so she's a myall lubra. But her brother can read and write.

Heather Dodd with Bruce and Susan Murray (circa 1958)

People from Arnhem Land used to come up there to Mainoru, as long as they got their families there. Sometimes old Jack used to kill a bullock for them and feed them up that way, and if they got little bit of money they'll come up and buy some tobacco. Oh, those days are gone. Things were not as dear as what they are now, you know. And then we used to get some of them to cut wood and clean round the house you know, then get everyone a bit of flour, tea, sugar and tobacco and things like that. They'd have a feed, and then they'd go off again.

Then the school started to come up now with all the kids come up to the house, running around. Jack McKay was asleep and then the kids running around, playing ball and waking him up.

Old Jack McKay never got married. He didn't want to be married. Oh, but he used to go into town and he said, 'Oh, come on Tex, let's go in town.'

Racism

Among pastoralists there is a tradition of hostility to government policies aimed at improving the lot of Aboriginal workers. The attitude of new managers and owners who come and go on neighbouring stations is unpredictable, but very few have been supportive and friendly towards the Aboriginal community at Bulman. Often the owners have not allowed Aboriginal people access to the station at all, let alone to the graves of their ancestors. In some cases they have been aggressively hostile, though more usually they are simply uncooperative and discouraging.

OP rum. It used to be called State Express. I used to go with him and they're the ones taught me how to drink.

He died at Mainoru [in 1966], and then they sold that place. We tried hard for Heather to get married and don't sell Mainoru. To keep it for Aborigine people, so they can live there. They been born there. We tried hard but when Jack McKay died, it was a heavy, heavy debt you know.

You know there was a big downfall there. All the Aboriginal people, Rembarrnga people mixed with Ngalakan, they worked there at Mainoru for long, long time. If Heather Dodd would of married—we wanted her to marry somebody and keep that Mainoru going for the Aboriginal people, it would've been good.

My father died there too. And old Mrs McKay, Jack's mother, died there. They all buried there in the yard. Just like that, you know. Nobody seems to look after it. I don't know why, they just don't. Where can we get in touch with someone that can go and clean it up and put a tombstone, or tomb, or something like that?

18. MY OLD DAD, JIMMY CAMFOO

My old man Jimmy Camfoo was walking somewhere, on the road from Mataranka to Alice, and he asked this miner bloke for a drink of water. The miner kicked him out because he was married to a gin [Aboriginal woman]. So then he went down to Alice Springs there and bought a camel and he used to take kids out for rides on the camel. Charged them sixpence for a ride, or sevenpence or something like that. And gradually he made some money. And then he went and bought the miner out, the bloke that kicked him out from the mine.

Maybe Hatches Creek, it was somewhere round there he bought the place off him. Old dad stuck to his work, and was getting good gold too, and the government wanted to buy the mine off him at their price. He said, 'No way in the world! If I ask a certain price you have to give me the certain price.'

But he had to be kicked out, he had to sell at the price the government offered. You know, whether he didn't like it or not, well, not for the price he was asking. So anyhow, then he went down Alice Springs and had a bit of a saddle shed there. He bought a shop, and he started off saddling then. He was a professional saddler. He worked for R.M. Williams [Australian bush outfitters]. Well he was going around and my young brother Jimmy, when he had grew up, he come to be a saddler too. Dad taught him you know. Old dad used to go out in the cattle stations. They would fix saddles up for them and pack-bags and pack-saddles and all these leather things and this dead brother of mine, young Jimmy, he used to do their housework. Then they'd go back home. He was a good saddler too. My dad never taught me to do saddle, but I picked it up on my own.

He made brand new saddles and things like this. You got all the different kinds of leather to do all this. I can do that too but I haven't got the machines. I got tools, like for the hand jobs. That's the best, you see, if you do it the right way.

And anyhow, he used to work right through Mainoru. He built that yard at Mainoru and he built the yard at Urapunga and he put a well down there and he put that fence running down Yellawater. Some of the old posts are still there. Right down at Yellawater!

All the Daniel family, Dennis and their father Daniel, used to work for my old dad. They used to do them on a contract. He never used to do work on wages, only contract. Well, for thirty bob a week, that was good money those days. You could buy a good pocket knife for sixpence or eightpence or something like that. You buy a pocket knife now, it's sixty-one, sixty-six dollars, some of them. I got big mob of pocket knife here. I ordered them from down Queensland, for my gear.

Anyhow my old dad made me go to school when he came to Roper Valley. I didn't want school, I wanted to go and play with the other kids, like Jack Gibb, Jimmy Gibb's son. And Ginger, just Ginger, he was head stockman. In those days they didn't have any names, only culture names, language names.

Jack Gibb was my best friend. We used to go out Roper Valley. 'Hey go and ask dad if we can borrow the .22 to go and shoot cockatoo or galah.' And we'd go down the creek and make a fire and cook it.

My dad asked me lessons and if I didn't know he would grab me and hang me up in the tree. He'd put me in a big sack bag in running water, 'I'll teach you, you little mongrel.' He'd tie a rope and put me up in a tree. Just that much in the water and my bum used to get wet. I'd be crying like anything. 'Stay there you little bastard.'

That's my father Jimmy Camfoo! That was when I was going around with my father and he used to do contract with old George Conway and old Jimmy Gibb. That happened at a place called Tullawar. That's how rough he was. I was like Dennis the Menace. In the morning my mother used to take me away. 'Come on my boy. Let's go bush. I don't want to live with that man there. I'll killim that man.'

And then he disappeared and I was taken over to Groote Eylandt. Anyhow later on, he stayed in Alice Springs there. Then he was too old and then he started to get the shakes and all that. He went to the Native Affairs there and asked, 'I want my son to come up.'

Anyhow my father he started to get the shakes because he was an opium smoker. He couldn't hardly talk properly and he said, 'Ah, I think I'll be gone soon.'

He wrote me a letter. Well he got the Native Affairs to write me a letter. 'Come and see dad. Dad wants you very urgent.'

I was just taking a mob of bullocks into Mataranka. So, Sandy McKay was a cook for me, and he took them to Mataranka and he said to me, 'What do you think? You still want to go down?'

'Oh, I'd better go see the old bugger.'

Sandy had some money so I got my wages. One old fella from Tennant Creek, he got his own private transport cart and stuff, to Darwin and back. I got on that one. Only me and him. We went down, but oh goodness, I felt like walking back. We camped this side of Tennant Creek, night time and early in the morning we were cold. We were COLD. Just as well we had a bottle of rum there, you know. Warm, warm your blood up.

And anyhow, we pulled in at Tennant Creek and went into his shop, with his wife and family and had breakfast there.

'Well, that's as far as I can help you.'

'No, that's not right. I'll have to find my own way.' I was very near to coming back from there.

'No', he said, 'you're here now. You might as well go on.'

I didn't know dad's mate was there at Tennant Creek. He had a little *gundi* [hut] there, on his own. I walked around there, didn't know anybody. And I went back to the same bloke again. He said, 'No, no, I couldn't find anybody to take you. You might have to grab a taxi. You see that old tin hut there, go there, that's where your dad was, he used to live there, he might be still there.'

So I walked over and was standing there and this old fella come out. He said, 'Hey, what can I do for you?'

I said, 'I'm named Jimmy Camfoo.'

'What? Your father was here about three days ago! He was here an' we usually camp here together. My mate.'

'Ah well, I come down to see him.'

'Yeah, he was talking about you. What are you going to do?'

'I don't know. I haven't got a car.'

'Here, here's about sixty pounds, here, you go and get a cab.'

He gave me sixty pounds.

'Oh well, old dad will pay you back!'

Anyhow I went around to one bloke, and he said, 'Oh, yeah, I'll drive you down. It'll cost about thirty-five pounds.'

Thirty-five quid, or forty pounds. He took me to Alice Springs and we got there somewhere about three or four o'clock in the morning. He said, 'Well I can't tell you. I don't know where to go.'

'Oh well, neither do I,' I said. 'I don't know where I am.'

'So, I'll just dump you down here at the creek here.'

'Yeah, that'll do. I'll go in there and have some sleep.'

I went down and I just slept and all of a sudden, birds start yelling. Daylight. And I'm sitting up, but I was only about from here to the road away from my father! But I didn't know. I walked around and found big mob of dark boys. They said, 'No, we don't know him.'

'Oh, well.'

I walked back again. I was sitting down smoking and this boy come up. 'Good morning. Well where you from?'

'I'm from Territory, up Katherine way. I'm looking for my father, Jimmy Camfoo.'

'You Camfoo?'

'Yeah, I'm trying to find my father.'

'Well you see that hut over there, that's where he is!'

He was over that road, you could see it, so close! Anyhow, I rolled my swag up and I walked around the place looking. I see another bloke's followed me from behind, one dark boy. So I walked slowly and he caught up with me. 'Excuse me. You know where's Jimmy Camfoo?'

'Yeah, I know.'

'Yeah, well that's my father. Can you take me to him? You know where?'

'Yeah, back there, same place. Yeah, I'll take you there.'

So I rang a cab, I give him some money then for a full flagon, and I got off there. I walked in and there he is, my dad. He looked at me and said, 'That you son?'

Anyhow, he was had it. He couldn't walk. I stayed there for two nights or three nights. Him and another bloke, they went fifty-fifty for one house. Good house too, stone house. Then he had an old jalopy. This car was there too, ready to be done up. We talked together. I run into a young bloke that dad grew up, Danny Goodwin. I call him brother too. Somewhere along the line he's a relation to Jimmy Camfoo. I had him out here working once.

I got a car there, so I went up to this mechanic who was a mate of Danny Goodwin. I said, 'Could you do that vehicle up?'

'Yeah, no worries. Only take about an hour to do it up.'

So we got packed up here next day and carried old dad out. It was a tray top, a pommy made thing. I didn't like it at all. But anyhow we put a drum of benzine, petrol on top and a drum of water. We put a bed there for him, mattress and everything, put a cover over him, it was cold. So we left. We camped half way. In the morning we got up and away we went. Just at Barrow Creek, I was driving and something happened and I tipped the vehicle.

This bloke sitting alongside me, he was asleep, and I was driving along you know, just coming around the corner. And these pommy made vehicles, they got big back and little engine in front, the four cylinder one. When I hit the bump, the front lifted up and I tried to swing around, follow the bend round you know and the front was up like this, off the bitumen.

It went off the road, and this bloke 'Agghhh...!!' he sang out. He grabbed the wheel and turned the wheel too. And it did one roll on its back and dad just fell straight onto the ground. I'm the only one got hurt. I lost one of my teeth. My leg was stuck in the door. They pulled me out. Copper come up and said, 'I'll leave it here now. I'll get a bloke I know here to take it to Tennant Creek.'

'I was drivin.''

'Oh, you were driving. And what's your name?'

'Camfoo.'

'Oh, Camfoo? You're one of the Camfoos? I know your dad well!'

And he's right there, laying there on the ground.

'I know him pretty well,' the policeman said, 'I don't think he'll hear about it. I'll give you a vehicle, I'll give you a car to take you down to Tennant Creek.'

Anyhow I got a car, and we were all packed in that car and he was drunk too, that bloke driving. Anyhow we got to Tennant Creek. 'Oh, well give him twenty pound. Twenty pound, that'll do. Enough to buy him a flagon, payment.'

We got there night-time. Early in the morning we said, 'What we gonna do?'

Dad, he wrote a cheque out, he had some money too. He could afford another vehicle if he wanted it. Anyhow, we got a cab from there to Mataranka. Got another cab from there to Katherine. We went to one of them Hayes mob, Francis Hayes' mother, Teresa Hayes. They had a house there. We went there and camped one night and in the morning I rang Nelly up. 'I'll be home on the mail plane.'

So I asked Teresa to look after the old man there, while I go back and get everything ready for dad in Mainoru.

I went to Mainoru. In about a week's time dad ended up there. He was there for maybe about four months, five months, but he couldn't walk. He couldn't walk, but I had to lead him to the toilet, or to the shower. He had a good little house there. I had to go, me and Tiga, had to go to Darwin. I had to go for a check-up too. And I got a bad news then, he died on Nelly's lap. Then we buried him with old Jack. Oh no, Jack was still alive then. We buried dad on the same place where old Mrs McKay was and where Jack is now.

Over the years I suffered a lot. I lost my mother and my dad and I didn't know till the last that he was dying at Mainoru. Sometimes I say it's good job the bastard's dead, he gave me a hard time I tell you when I didn't go to school and couldn't read. He hung me up in the tree!

After he bought that place in Alice Springs he had a lot of kids. I don't know all my brothers, sisters. Everyone knows me if I get down there. My brother Dean Camfoo, he was as black as the ace of spades. He was always humbugging for money, wanted to buy a motor car. He's got a place there and it's made of gold, he's got lots of money. He says come to my place, but I say it's too cold, I'll stay up at my country.

19. PERMISSION TO MARRY

There's a few of us, really, Mick Daly, Billy Fulton, George Moroni and myself, who were going to marry to Aboriginal women. They gave us three years of trouble. You had to wait three years to find out if you could marry because they wanted to be sure. They gave us three years of waiting. They might say that they wanted to be sure.

This bloke, Mick Daly, he was a good drover. He had a beautiful Aboriginal girl. Native Affairs got him and took him to court and fine him big. But he kept fighting them for it. It took him three years but eventually he got married. And he married a beautiful girl, but she become a drinker. He might be died, this old fella now. I met him many a time. Well it's just the same with me but I was more little bit lucky, you know.

Old Jack and Native Affairs and coppers and everything, they knew I was going with Nelly. For four or five years we went around and she was on my mind, that young girl. After a while they found out. They went and seen Billy Fulton too. He was going to marry Rosie. And George Moroni, they married, but he and his wife, they parted. And I was the only one that stuck, although with all the rows and heartaches we can get.

Anyhow then, well Jack McKay wouldn't help me and Nelly. Jimmy Dodd wouldn't help. They didn't want to be mixed up in it. So we pulled out and went to Mountain Valley. Ray Hood helped us then to fill out all the forms. That minister come out and saw us. They were going to take a long time. They wanted to find out really if me and Ruth are married. But they found out that we weren't officially married then. Policeman came out to talk about it. They couldn't do anything. There

> **Marriage**
>
> Marriages were forbidden between Aborigines and whites, except with the permission of the Director of Native Affairs, so many relationships had an air of illegitimacy. Europeans who had been granted a permit to marry a 'lubra' or a 'half-caste' were placed on a list which was supplied to police. But many men who were unofficially categorised 'half-caste' did not know whether they were required to have permission to marry a 'lubra'. Sometimes such men wrote to the Director of Native Affairs requesting permission to marry a 'full-blood' woman, only to be told they did not require a permit because they were themselves subject to the Aboriginal Ordinance. Others who were exempt or had not been listed as Wards had to have a 'permit to marry' an Aboriginal woman.

wasn't a leg to stand on. Even the ministers, they knew I wasn't officially married to Ruth. It was a Christian marriage according to the missionary, but it wasn't a legal one.

I don't know why, but they didn't like white man mucking around with dark girls. Maybe fine, or six months in gaol. You had to write a letter to ask. Then they got to follow your background and things like that. It takes a long while. It's not worth it, so some of them they just live with them and then after a while they might kick her out there. Well that's why they've got to be sure of that man.

Anyhow after a while we went to Katherine. We worked there. Nelly worked in the hospital and I was cutting wood you know. I used to cut wood for town at the sawmill. It was up the hospital there. After a while I went back to Mainoru again. I left Nelly there, at the hospital working and I was working at Mainoru again. Head stockman. I got four hundred bullocks with Jack and I took them into town. And Ray Hood come out and said, 'Oh, that Reverend Lang is there.' Finally they'd run into Reverend Lang in Mataranka.

'Oh, you gotta come up to Katherine. Reverend Lang there, now he gonna marry you. You and Nelly gonna get married in Katherine.'

So we delivered those cattle, the bullocks, at Mataranka. I jumped on the train there, up to Katherine. In the morning that bloke come up, say, 'Oh, you better come up now. Old Minister already there.'

We went up there, just a private place. But Dr Moo was our best man and Mrs Ryan, that's Ron Ryan, the patrol officer's wife. She took the wedding ring. I didn't have any. We didn't have any money to get a ring. We put it on us and that's it. We sign the paper and Ron Ryan said, 'You try and get away now!'

They took my photos and everything like that. 'You never run away now!'

I was hobbled!

Ever since then we worked there. We never left Mainoru until Jack McKay sold the place.

6. LOVE AND MARRIAGE

Tex saw me before, at Larrimah, when I was a young girl. He didn't forget me. He was asking for me everywhere. He was married then, at Ngukkur. Then he came one time to Mainoru and found me and we stayed there for twenty years. Because we were married, Christian marriage, proper marriage, with the Church in Katherine. Presbyterian, Church of England. That's same one isn't it? Our Minister was Mr and Mrs Father Reverend Mayne. Our best man was a Chinaman, Dr Moo [well-known Northern Territory eye surgeon]. He died. He was the first doctor in Katherine. He had a boy and two girls. He was a really good doctor. I used to work for him for one year before I got married. His wife was my bridesmaid.

But before that, Tex had really big trouble, because in those days we weren't citizens yet. The Welfare wouldn't let us marry half-caste men or whitefella men. Once they wanted to catch me red-handed. They rode a donkey to pick Tex up. They hid the saddle and tracked us in bush. But they didn't catch me and Tex.

Then policeman and all they came out [to Mainoru] and questioned me. 'Did you muck around [have sex] with that boy?'

I said 'Yes'. I didn't tell a lie. I wasn't frightened. The police came out and asked me again and again. I said, 'If you going to put Tex in gaol I can't help it because I'm in love with him. What do you do if you're in love with your girlfriend and you're engaged and live with them for some time? Well you know, love is love.'

They called me to the table and I said, 'Well you can't stop my love. If you going to take Tex to gaol you might as well put me in too.'

I thought we'd get a letter and get summonsed. I thought they were going to say six months in gaol because you muck around with one another. But he got one mail and I got one mail, engagement paper. 'You are entitled to go with your girlfriend in town now.' I suppose they think, 'We can't stop her because that girl's too smart.' They couldn't catch me.

The wife of the Welfare [patrol officer] made my dress, she dressed me. Tex went one way, I went another. You know how you do it. A few Aboriginal people were at our wedding but nearly all whitefellas. Mr Ryan the Welfare man was saying, 'I'm handing Nelly to Tex Camfoo.'

And Mrs Ryan gave me the biggest ring. I couldn't fit it. They got another one for me from Darwin. I was really spoiled girl in one way, but one way I made a lot of trouble for Mr Giese [Director of Welfare]. He won't forget me, that Mr Giese. He always say, 'By golly Nelly and Tex, you can get me in a lot of trouble.'

Welfare

Mr Harry Giese was the Director of Welfare in the Northern Territory between the years of 1953 and 1972. He was appointed by Paul Hasluck then Minister for Territories in the Liberal government in Canberra to implement new policies of training Aborigines and assimilating them into white society. These policies were then seen as positive and progressive. Like the Director of Native Affairs before him, Giese wielded considerable direct power over individual Aboriginal lives.

Mr Harry Giese (late 1950s)

Photo: Courtesy of the Museum and Art Gallery of the Northern Territory

20. THE DOG TICKET

Full wages started to come from that time. Jack McKay paid them ten bob a week. Probably before that they used to work for stick of tobacco. I was mustering around with all the boys, all these old fellas, at Puppydog we camped there. I used to carry a little wireless and I heard that news. Now all the Aboriginal people are citizens. They can go in the pub and drink. They are just the same as white man. I said, 'Come on, quick, quick, come on!'

When they hear that, 'Oh, let's go the pub, drink!' What they are now, spoilt.

You couldn't drink before. We had to get a little 'dog ticket'. We used to call it 'dog ticket', little exemption card, you know. Keep that in our pocket all the time. When you go in, you have to show that to the bar man. Well, if that publican asks you if you are allowed, you can say, 'Yeah, I got my exemption card.'

Then you got to show it to them or they go and have a look at the noticeboard they got there, with all the half-casts for all the exemptions.

If you were an Aboriginal ringer you couldn't drink. But our friend used to go and get it for us. We meet along the river somewhere or go out bush and drink. If any white man get caught they got a heavy fine, heavy fine or six months in gaol. We didn't get fined.

Whatever job we used to do, the Native Affairs got two bob out of it. Two bob, you know, because they were fighting for us and looking after the Aboriginal people, in that sort of way. So that's how

> **Drinking**
>
> Because it was taken for granted that Tex was an *Aboriginal* ringer, he had not been allowed to go to the pub with the white stockmen he worked with. The authorities had then decided that Tex was not Aboriginal because his father was Chinese. As a result of a national referendum in 1967 Aborigines gained what is called 'citizenship rights'. The most obvious change was that they were given the right to drink alcohol, and thus many people in the Northern Territory equated citizenship with the right to go into the pub.
>
> Tex' sense of citizenship having 'spoilt' Aboriginal people is an example of the ambivalence many Aboriginal people express about these historical conditions, especially in the form of nostalgia for what is now seen as a more simple past.

the Native Affairs were put on for that sort of job, to look after Aboriginal people and their troubles and things like that.

And court. Native Affairs used to go up to court and talk to them you know, to look after the Aboriginal people. It was like the Legal Aid now. They used to be sent out to Aboriginal settlements to talk about things. I think they used to take them in court and talk up for them. Like, 'We are here to help you. You just tell us the reason why you got picked up.'

Native Affairs Branch

Under the Aboriginal Ordinance, the Director of Native Affairs was in charge of all Aboriginal people and had the responsibility of ensuring that conditions on the cattle stations were in accordance with the law. In the early days, 'native' workers' wages were paid to the Chief Protector to be held in trust. Aboriginal employees could then ask the Protector, who was the patrol officer or the policeman, for some money.

In the 1950s the stations had to provide accommodation, food, clothing and payment to their Aboriginal workers. Until 1968, wages were well below that of white workers and only part of Aboriginal wages had to be paid in cash. The rest was paid into the Aboriginal Benefits Trust Fund, with the intention that it would be spent to improve the living conditions of Aborigines. This fund was later used to promote self-determination and to provide resources for outstations.

21. STOCKMEN and LANDOWNERS

In some places there was Aboriginal head stockmen with white men under them. Like at Roper Valley they had one bloke called Yarramanek—he had a kink in the neck that's why he's called that. He's Power Jack's brother. He used to take me over sometimes. He was a head stockman. White man used to work under him at Roper Valley.

Then after, there was Blitzer, he run the camp there for a while and then after that, old George Jardaku. I used to go and meet him at the southern boundary and me and him used to muster up there on the boundary and go half and half in cleanskins. They were good head stockmen there. Aboriginal stockmen were leading because they taught a lot of Europeans how to muster and all that too. They were mighty ringers and horsemen and some of them come to be head stockmen in some places.

When we started off here at Bulman I was the one that started this place off. We were living just here when you first come out that time [1975/76]. Well I was managing the station here then.

Well, when I started off, I started off good because I learned when I was young you know. I worked as a jackaroo for George Conway. And he was a rough man. He couldn't read or write. But he taught me how to run the cattle and how to work cattle and things like that. I was just a jackaroo, and after a while then I come to be a stockman. Well I had to go about three years straight of jackarooing and just about two, three years as a stockman. Then I come to be head stockman. After that I come to be an overseer. Then I become a manager for Gulperan, you know. I couldn't do books properly. But I still passed all my trade certificates at Nutwood Downs when I run Number Two camp.

> **Black bosses**
>
> White men rarely worked under brown men, let alone black men. However in the 1970s government funding of Aboriginal enterprises, including a cattle station at Ngukurr, meant that black men became bosses.
>
> **Naming**
>
> The name Bulman was conferred by whites for the whole area. The name Gulperan was chosen by the government officials for the pastoral company because Gonjimbi, the name of the locality, was too difficult to pronounce and spell. Gulin Gulin was the name conferred after the Gulperan bankruptcy (see page 94). Thus bureaucratic requirements still influence naming practices in Aboriginal communities.

There was quite a lot of boys, about fifteen stockman! I was running Number Two camp and well Jimmy Wesley, he was a coloured boy too, he run the Number One camp.

*   *   *

Old Billy Moore, he was like me, half-caste. He owned Mountain Valley one time. He was a gun stockman, that bloke. They took a mob of bullocks down Mataranka and he got drunk up there with Ray and the Hood brothers. Billy sold it for a song. Sold Mountain Valley Station for a song. They give him an old jalopy. I don't know how much money they paid for it. It was worth about fifteen, twenty thousand dollars at the time. He had over a thousand head of cattle. Everybody said he sold it for a song. If he wouldn't have sold it he would've been sitting pretty.

You know, it was all good cattle country and there was cattle all over the place. He had Mainoru this side. Beswick on the other side, Roper Valley on the southern side. There was a lot of cattle those days, because there was not many stations around. No Moreoak then.

Jack McKay helped Billy Moore to get Mountain Valley. He used to work with Jack, one season, like half a season, muster round here, and get a lot of bullocks for him. Take them to town to sell it. Then come back, two weeks holiday. Then Mainoru used to go and muster at his place. Give him a hand to muster because he didn't have many boys, you know. They used to work the two stations together. Well, one after the other, like work at Mainoru then go back to Mountain Valley and round all his calves and maybe sell ten or thirty steers you know, to make some money. He was doing all right but he couldn't read or write either. Anyway he sold it in the end.

22. RODEO AND RACES

We used to have rodeo, every year. We used to come into Katherine. We are the ones who started it off really. All the bushmen you know. We used to get together from Mainoru. Jack used to take me and Bandicoot. We were the riders from Mainoru. There were lot of young boys from Mountain Valley, and Ray Hood and Neville Hood, two brothers, they used to go and ride too. There wasn't much money those days, like for rodeo. It was good money down south in Queensland. Well, not as good as they having now. I remember, I won the buck championship. Open buck championship. I come in the third round. Neville was in front, and then Bandicoot was second and then I come third. I only won about couple of dollars, I mean a couple of pounds.

The bushmen from up this area, we started that rodeo off. One day it was rodeo, then the next day a horse final for the best rider. Me and Neville and Bandicoot were in that too. Well I was the last one, I didn't get anywhere.

Anyhow, that's how it started then. This Jack Gill Brothers, the travelling rodeo, used to come around, where Kirby's is now, just straight out where Randazzo Terrace is. There was no town in there yet and that's where they used to rig their tent up. I went up and rode there too, but I never won anything. You ride no stirrups, they take the stirrups out, and a halter to hold. They used to bring the buckjumpers and bull ride and all that, but inside a tent. The tent as big as, or twice as big as this house. A big tent and they used to have a yard inside there and we used to ride in there. Old Jack McKay used to come

Tex Camfoo buckjumping at Mainoru (mid 1950s)

Photo: Courtesy of the Museum and Art Gallery of the Northern Territory

and pay for my fee. Then we would go and ride. We couldn't drink because we never had citizenship then, but we used to get our beers, somehow.

Old Jack, he was a real drinker. Apparently I learned from him. He was a good boss. He was good with Aboriginal ways, like helping Aboriginal people. And so was all the McKay family. They all good people. They loved Aboriginal people. They used to work with them and look after them and things like that at Mainoru, and well, we had a good time when the McKay mob were there.

Well one time from Mainoru we said, 'Oh let's, let's have a race meeting.'

Just after you pass Bulman turn-off, there's a big plain in there. Nothing but ant bed. We called it Turkey Plain. It was lousy with turkeys. We used to have bit of a race meeting there. All the Hoods mob from Mountain Valley and the Mainoru mob. I'd send my horses there, station horses, like I was head stockman. And the Hood brothers used to bring their racehorses and we would have a big meeting there. Alma and old Lucy and Florry and all, they used to ride there too. Three days meeting it was. That was the good old days.

Bandicoot Robinson at Katherine rodeo (1953)

Photo: Courtesy of the Museum and Art Gallery of the Northern Territory

23. WHITEFELLA, BLACKFELLA?

To tell you the truth, I feel both ways, European and blackfella. I can't help it, because I got bit of mixed blood in me. Chinaman, Aboriginal, and blackfella. Well, I go into town, they respect me as a European, because, well I don't talk *very* good English, but I talk like, good English. Sometimes I can't because I mix bit of pidgin English in there too. I couldn't help being that way, because I'm proud to be the way I am.

Sometimes they reckon, they call me a black bastard, sometimes in the pub like, you know. I just laugh at it, I just sometimes say, 'I'm proud of it.'

We might have a different colour, but same blood. But it doesn't worry me. I just answer that back. I say, 'You're a white bastard too. What's the difference?'

Sometimes little bit, like, sort of make me shame when they do say that sort of thing, but it doesn't affect me. I'm proud to be an Aborigine. 'I can't help it. You're to blame for it! You know, you've been knocking around with my mother, that's why I come out a bloody yellafella. That's your blame!'

And they just shut up like a book then.

'I can't help it.' That's what I say.

24. CHRISTMAS

Old Jack McKay had an old International truck. Once a month he used to go into town and take old Chuckaduck, or old Larry, and old Dick and load up with food and fuel and things and come back again on that old road that goes right down Flying Fox, Kielly, Sugarbag, Moreoak, Bucket Creek, on the old road and nearly all black soil country. Do that again in another three or four weeks time. Old Jack McKay used to say, 'I'll go into town an' get us Christmas supplies.'

We never used to have Christmas at the right time. We always had it about two weeks after because he was bogged out of sight. He'd go and get a few beers and OP rum, State Express. Then Jimmy Dodd would ring up the Cox' shop in Katherine, 'Jack left yet?'

Heather Dodd, Nelly Camfoo and Colin MacKenzie standing beside the old International truck at Mainoru (circa 1962)

'Oh, he left about, oh, four days ago!'

'Oh, he'll be halfway home now.'

Old Jimmy Dodd would say, 'Right oh, pack your gear up and get tucker and we'll go and look for him.'

And it took us about couple of days before we'd get to Jack. There he is, bogged down, laying down, with a bottle of rum at his side there. He told us, 'Have a nip.'

Then me and Jimmy Dodd we end up getting drunk with all this Christmas supplies on board. They're waiting for us for Christmas!

It would take us another two days to get home, pulling one another across the bog. I used to love it you know, in my young days. When we got there, 'He's all in one piece. Half of the beer's gone!'

One time when he left he said, 'I'll be back probably Christmas Eve.'

He never come. Well he couldn't get back because he got bogged. Anyhow me and Jimmy Dodd went out, and another bloke. There he was, laying down, waiting for help. He knew that we would come looking. It took us two days before we got to him. Anyway it took us about three days to get home from there. It was only about sixty miles out, but it took us three days to get home. Oh, water all over the place. Some places, we used to have half a day putting timber across the bog-hole so they can get across. Luckily we had two vehicles: the old International and he had a Connel three tonner. Three ton of stock on board.

One time he run out of oil. So he said to the boy, 'Go out and get a bullock. It's got to be a fat bullock or fat cow.'

Well they got one and boiled all the fat and he rendered the fat and mixed it up for oil. Pour it down the engine and he got home. He used to come back tied up with wire, all broken parts, like springs and things like that. Tied up with a piece of Cobb & Co. We used to call it that.

There's a song about old Jack McKay and his OP rum by Ted Egan.

> Oh, they've got some bloody good drinkers in the Northern Territory,
> From Darwin down to Alice Springs they're always on a spree,
> From out on the Barkly Tableland and across to V.R.D., [Victoria River Downs]
> They've got some bloody good drinkers in the Northern Territory.
>
> Jack McKay used to measure the bogs on the road to Mainoru,
> By the number of bottles of OP rum it'd take him to drink his way through,
> His best was a twenty seven bottler, in a wet when you'd bog a duck,
> But it didn't worry Jack on the Mainoru track, he kept bellowin' out: 'Good Luck'.
>
> Oh, the drinkers of the Territory are black and brown and white,
> But no matter what your colour is you get into it every night,
> So grab yourself a stubby and sing along with me,
> About those bloody good drinkers in the Northern Territory.
>
> See Ted Egan, *Sit Down Up North*, 1997, pp. 94–96.

*   *   *

One time, we were coming back with big mob of loads, a lot of people sitting on the back, and me and him in front there, driving away, having a few grog, grog all the way.

'Hey go on, open it up!'

'Oh we should go through that OP rum, State Express, 222.'

Oh, goodness, I tell you, your hair stands on your head!

Anyway, we come down to Mywok Creek. I don't know how the body of the truck never fell off half way, but it did there, right in the middle of the river. Luckily, the river wasn't running. It was only dead, dry river. All of the tray on the back including the rations, all the stuff that we had there including the people that were sitting on the back, we left them on the bed of the river. And Jack said, 'Oh where's our mob, where's our truck?'

I told him, 'There, there they are. In the middle of the river there, sitting there up on the tray.'

Luckily it wasn't running. They shout, 'Hey boss! Hey boss! Pull up! Pull up! Pull up!'

And it took us nearly two days to unload and carry all the stuff and we built it back again with Cobb & Co. Oh I couldn't help laughing you know. We were held up for another two, three days.

When old Jack died, he was broke you know. All the bills to pay. That's why they had to sell Mainoru, to pay the bills then. The bank more or less owned Mainoru.

25. PODDY DODGING

It was a funny sort of a turn-out with the boundaries. We used to notify Mountain Valley, our next-door neighbour, that we'd meet them in three days time or whatever, next week at the boundary. Muster along the boundary, and go half and half on cleanskins. We used to do that, maybe about five days muster or one week muster, and then we split up. They'd go back to Mountain Valley and we'd go back to Mainoru.

Sometimes they used to come poddy dodging round our area you know, and then I'd send boys to foot-walk. Give them couple of tins of tobacco, tea and sugar. 'You go Mywok and Mountain Valley and see if the Hood brothers still there.' They used to go and come back and give me the news that they not there, they mustering.

> **Poddy dodging**
>
> A 'poddy' is an unbranded or cleanskin calf. Poddy dodging was the widespread practice of mustering cleanskins on other people's leases and branding them with one's own brand. As many stations were unfenced, the boundaries and therefore the ownership of stock was often unclear, and poddy dodging was endemic.

'Oh, where they going?'

'Oh, this way, Sandy Creek or Top Yard way.'

I used to go around and, me and one boy Chuckaduck or old Left Hand, or Diver. I used to send them around. 'You go here. You there night-time and open the gates for them. Let all the cattle go.'

Oh all the sneaking things we used to do! We never used to worry about it. They muster or they take their mob or whatever cattle they get from Mainoru. Then I'd find out where they mustering. 'Oh they mustering out Beswick way.'

My turn now. I'd go and poddy dodge their country and take big mob of cleanskins back. Then we'd meet up and have a big fisty-cuff fight. Oh, big argument, especially when we'd meet up in Mataranka or races and all that. We used to fight then. The good old days.

The police never came unless someone complained to them, or someone saw them mustering inside our boundary. But otherwise, they didn't care.

If they catch you red-handed they will take everything off you. Only the branded cattle, or take the lot and put a court order. In the olden days time, early days, but not in my days.

Well Cowboy Collins, Ted Collins, we used to do the dirty work for him. When he sold Beswick he guaranteed that there were a little over two thousand head of cattle there. But he never had that much. The only way he could build that number up was by poddy dodging someone else's cattle. So we did that for him.

Anyhow, we mustered all the cattle including Mark O'Connor's Mataranka cattle and even Elsey Station, there on the southern side of Beswick. We mustered all that cattle, and built up the number. We had to cross-brand them then, you know, put our mark over that other one there. We were cross-branding anyone's cattle! This bloke Simms, Harry Simms, he was coming to manage Beswick. And he's sitting there counting the number, right at the crush where they go through the gate after they're branded. And poor bugger, we're laughing like anything you know. And after the last lot went through, 'Hey, hey! Pull up, pull up, pull up! What's that brand? What's that ear mark?'

They were too late, over two thousand head of stranger cattle was cross-branded. They had ear-marks. But he wasn't a cattleman. He didn't notice till the end. Well Cowboy Ted Collins was all right because he got his money from what he's selling—over three thousand head of cattle, that belongs to the next-door neighbour! I don't know how he got out of that. I worked for that head stockman at Beswick, Harry Simms. He used to muck around with Aboriginal girls too, although his wife was there.

When I worked at Beswick, our next-door neighbour was old Mark O'Connor. He owned Mataranka. Right where the old Mataranka homestead is, where the pub is now. We used to take three or four live bullocks down to Mataranka you know, to kill, for the pub. It was Ted Collin's cattle there but they didn't come up with the money for them. That Cowboy Collins, he'd rob his own mother. He told us, 'When you all go back, start from the boundary, mustering up to Beswick. You can brand some of the cattle.'

Well I was the head stockman. Anyhow, we mustered all the way right up to the wire yard. We camped there one night, and I had a terrible headache. So I said to the boys, 'You mob go up muster on the other side and come up and leave the cattle in the yard.'

And blow me dead if it wasn't Mark O'Connor comes up. Mark O'Connor and Jim Bellow and that Aboriginal boy that used to do all the work for him.

So he went up the yard, found two mickeys, young bulls, Beswick cattle, in with our cattle, in the yard. He said, 'Oh, how's it going Tex?'

'Oh, all right.'

'And what those two mickeys there, in amongst your cows?'

'Ah, we picked them up.'

'Oh, that's all right, no worries.'

But he reported me to the coppers you know, to the policeman. So, we went home and branded them and all that, and the next minute a letter comes saying for me to come in for a court case. But we got out of it. I rode in and went to the court. Cowboy Collins said, 'I'll talk for him.'

He said, 'Well you know a bull when it finds a cow, it'll keep pestering, and it won't run away. It wants to go back to her, you know. That's what happened. It wasn't Tex' fault.'

And we beat the case like that. It was about half an hour and I was let free.

26. LEAVING MAINORU

Sandy McKay, well he was a schoolteacher. He was around Snake Bay, Melville Island all through there. In school holidays he used to come up and work on Mainoru for a while to do the books. He used to come out and work with me, do the cooking out in the stock camp. When their mother died and Jack died, he didn't have much left. He worked at Beswick, school teaching there for short while. He was a sick man too, and apparently he died at Beswick.

And there was Jimmy Dodd, Mrs Dodd's husband. He was a pommy bloke. He was all right, he was, you know, a good old guy. I used to work with him before I got that head stockman job on Mainoru. All that paving work at the station there when they pulled one down and built another building on it. It was two Sydney William [iron frame] huts put together. I done all that floor work there for them.

Me, Willy Martin and Jimmy Dodd. He was just like we were working under him. And old Billy Lawrence, Laughlin's [Tex and Nelly's nephew] father. Well he died too, Billy. He was black. Oh, nice bloke too, my great friend. He used to work for me here. Anyhow, I did all that paving work for him, because that was my trade. I used to do lot of paving work at Roper, at Ngukurr.

After Jack McKay died they sold Mainoru to Revorse brothers. I kept working there until John Morrison come out to be manager there. He was a no-good bloke. I worked for him for a while. I didn't stay long, I pulled out. The Revorse brothers were American and they had Finnis River Station. And when I pulled out they rang up and said, 'Oh, leave Tex where he is. See what he's going to do.'

I hung on there for a while then they sent a message to go and work at Finnis River for them. So me and Nelly, we were married then, we went up and I was a horse tailer [the person who followed the spare horses and looked after them during mustering and droving]. Well not just a horse tailer, I was sort of a stockman and also, driver. Ship the gear from one place to the other. Nelly was the cook. We worked there for about three or four months. I didn't like them anyhow, they don't pay good money. So they rang and said, 'Oh, you have to go back. We'll send you back to Mainoru again.'

Well then they kicked Danny Morrison out and I didn't want to work then. Lee Revorse and his brother, they kicked him out because they reckon he was doing the wrong thing. Then they sent me and Nelly back and then another bloke they got there, he and I had a row. I pulled out from him and then I went back to Ngukurr again.

I worked there for a while at Urapunga. Worked for Ray Fryor. I was head stockman on a contract. I made a couple of thousand dollars in five to ten days. There was only three boys and Nelly cooking for us. I used to cook early, then go out mustering every day, you know, to tail coaches while we run the mob into the quiet cattle. Warren [Tex' son] was a little kid then. Nelly used to carry him in front of the saddle. When we ran wild cattle in to the coaches, we would put him up a tree till the cattle settled down. We made lot of money there, contracting, and then I decided to leave there. It was getting a bit hot, so I went back to Ngukurr to run the camp there for a while.

* * *

Around that time at Mainoru they chased the people out. Paddy Cavanagh was the white bloke there then. They chased all the Rembarrnga people who been living there for years, they chased them out. It was that American bloke, brought in from America, Foster. Paddy Cavanagh and Len Brody worked for him. They are the ones that kicked the people out from Mainoru. They followed them up all the way too, to see if they can find if they'd kill any cattle. But they only followed far as Lindsay Creek and that's where the sand ridge stops there at the Mainoru boundary. This side of Lindsay is all Arnhem Land.

They got plenty of meat all the way. They were walking in the blazing sun, hot weather. It took them about a week, or maybe just about two weeks to walk from there to Bulman waterhole. They had kids, goats and dogs and one was pregnant. Nelly's sister, Dolly, she was pregnant for Regina. Regina

Mainoru

Mainoru station was never very profitable and was in debt when sold in 1969 [see Gillian Cowlishaw, *Rednecks, Eggheads and Blackfellas*, 1999].

Refugees

Max Foster bought Mainoru from Heather Dodd in 1968. This was also the year in which Aborigines had to be paid equal wages. Since he wanted the minimum number of workers, the Aboriginal community was dispersed. A group of about twenty people finally and reluctantly left Mainoru on foot after Chuckaduck was threatened with a gun.

The Aborigines were afraid that the white managers wanted to catch them killing Mainoru cattle, a hangover from the earlier era when they were shot for such actions.

was born down the river here. Well I was at Ngukurr then and old Dick died at Mainoru.

They come up to Bulman and stop there, and then Danny Watson brought all his cattle back from Maningrida. They couldn't grow cattle at Maningrida because all the sand country, rotten country, no good for cattle. He said, 'You mind if we take these cattle back to Beswick?'

They asked that old fella, name of Singleton, Jimmy Singleton's father, from Maningrida. Anyhow, they come up here, they come to this place at Weemol and say, 'Oh this the place for me.'

They made a yard and tailed about three hundred head of cattle here. Then he found out that all the Rembarrnga people were down there at Bulman Waterhole, and he went and picked them up and brought them back here. Goats and all. Anyhow they started that place up then, Gulperan Pastoral Company. Where Warren's house is, that bit of concrete is still there. I was working at Roper and all of a sudden I got a letter, 'Tex, you interested in running a camp here at Bulman because you know this country?'

> **Refugees**
>
> Danny Watson was an experienced cattle man employed by the Department of Aboriginal Affairs (DAA) early in the self-determination era to manage Aboriginal cattle enterprises at Maningrida, at Bulman and then at Beswick. He encouraged the Aboriginal people to locate the new Gulperan Company at Bulman (Gonjimbi) where a small mining company had left some tin sheds and a bore water supply.

I took the job straight away. I rang up from Ngukurr, I rang up to VJY [call sign for the radio telephone] and said, 'Get the horses ready and I'll be there, in two or three days time.'

I got an old Land Rover. A big mob jumped on there, including my uncle Charlie. Dawson Daniels said, 'Oh I'll come too.' It was only the front wheels was working. The back one was all eaten out. And the fanwheels was all broken. But we ended up here and put the camp up straight away.

7. THEY DIDN'T WANT BLACKFELLA

They sold Mainoru station. Yankee came. We stayed there one time with a good Yankee. Then that good Yankee sold the station to another Yankee, the Foster family, and they're the ones who went hard. They just didn't like blackfella. They didn't want blackfella round Mainoru. Yanks were taking over, otherwise we could stay at Mainoru. But me and old man Tex, we went away. We were working at Gove and at Roper.

This mob here, they went away then. They walked from Mainoru and sat down [stayed] here at Bulman. They brought all the goats and their swag. Then this bloke named Danny Watson, he was with Welfare, working under a Welfare bloke named John Hunter. When he came here, starting where we are staying now, Danny Watson was fighting for Rembarrnga tribe. And John Hunter and the Welfare, the other Welfare, was fighting for the Maningrida

Nelly Camfoo tending Tex' foot at Gonjimbi, Bulman (1976)

Photo: Gillian Cowlishaw

mob. The Maningrida mob was going to come up here and stay here but Danny Watson used to say that this belongs to these people, tribal people.

Me and old Tex were at Roper, I was working at the school, cleaning. Danny Watson was waiting for us at Bulman. We came back then, and stopped here for good now. Danny Watson told us that he was going to start the Aboriginal station for us. When Welfare didn't want Danny to help us, he took all those cattle and horses to Beswick, to that other Welfare country.

After Danny Watson left, my old man [Tex] and my brother Willy, they went to Darwin with the directors who belong to this place. They asked Mr Giese for money from the ABTF [Aboriginal Benefits Trust Fund] to start up a station. We came back and started it then. We bought horses from other stations and we bought breeders, and one Brahman bull. We worked and made this country big.

This is Ngalpon country, and Rembarrnga. Rembarrnga grew it up, worked it up, and made it higher [more valuable]. We were making it big, this country. That place where we camped before, Gonjimbi, *mununga* called it Gulperan Pastoral Company. Now we've got this Gulin Gulin. Why they changed this place is because this country owed DAA [Department of Aboriginal Affairs] a big debt.

27. MANAGING GULPERAN PASTORAL COMPANY

After Danny Watson was sent to Beswick I was head stockman. I went to Beswick to see Mr Giese. He came up there and we had a bit of a talk. He said 'Tex, you've got twenty-five thousand dollars here. Do you want it? I was going to keep it for my own.' He handed the cheque to Danny Watson and the cheque went up to Darwin. I used that to open this place up again for stock, cattle, horses, saddles and bridles. We got them from Mountain Valley, from Bill somebody, who managed the station. We started off like that. For the wages, the accountant in Darwin had two way radio and I'd call the names and say how many are working, how much they're getting and he sent out money by plane for the working men. I only had two or three to start.

At one time we thought they were going to close this place down, this Bulman. We got a letter from Mr Giese in Darwin, and he said, 'It looks like Bulman's going to be closed, so what about you two go to Darwin and try to talk to Bill Frazier from the Welfare.'

He was an ex-copper, he was a big boss in Darwin. Me and Mick Painter caught a plane to Darwin. We used the money we saved here. We had this meeting with Bill Frazier and two or three other men. He said, 'It looks like we can open that place up again, but before we do that we're gonna get rid of some of the buffalo, because there's too many buffalo here to start a cattle station.'

We talked for half a day.

There were hundreds on the old airstrip there. Then we put it in the paper that we wanted a

---

Self-determination

In the 1970s the Australian government began to fund Aboriginal commercial enterprises as part of a self-determination policy. White managers were appointed by a firm of pastoral consultants and the Department of Aboriginal Affairs. The policy assumed literacy, numeracy and an understanding of funding guidelines and business practices. It also assumed that 'the community' as a whole wanted to transform themselves into 'modern' men and women, and abandon their own cultural heritage: language, kinship, ceremony, beliefs. Misunderstandings, embarrassment and humiliation were common, sometimes leading to disillusionment and resistance.

The Gulperan Pastoral Company was set up in 1972, but was bankrupt and abandoned by the early 1980s. During the 1970s there was a good deal of mismanagement of this and other ventures, due to poor planning, changing bureaucratic rules, and white managers with varying levels of expertise and honesty. The Aborigines' limited literacy and experience with money, bureaucracy, management and accountability led to them being blamed for many financial disasters.

buffalo contractor and Colin Howells started the abattoir, about sixty thousand dollars worth of abattoir, down at the flat where the garage is now. I don't know how he pulled the big freezers and all that. They had caravans and everything. That was after the Western Nuclear mining mob left. They started work putting up the killing place and freezers and big generator and all that. It took them about two or three weeks to put it all up. They made it so they had a contract for three years, in 1972 or 1973.

We used to get about two or three thousand dollars a fortnight from the buffalo. That wasn't wages, it was royalties. We never had much, we never used to go for motor cars and things like that. We killed beef there for human consumption, for sale overseas. Colin Howell had a contract here for three years, but he didn't go that far because the Katherine abattoirs was closed. That contract lasted three years but he only went two and a half years. He should've went three years with the abattoirs but he had enough money to pull out. But instead of leaving all the equipment for us like it said in the contract, he dragged all his things away and left. Then he wanted to come back and we said, 'No, you never come back here again.'

He should've done the right thing you know. But he was a fair man. He paid his boys good money: two thousand dollars cash every fortnight. They had their own butcher shop, killing floor. Well they used to kill outside and bring it in and butcher them right on the spot. And the freezing company used to come from Katherine nearly every week. That was buffalo. From just around here, around the fence, around the strip, right where the station is, around Weemol. We killed about nine and a half thousand buffalos, in that time.

*   *   *

We got Peter Hannath for the manager when Gulperan started to build up. He was working in Africa somewhere before, Kenya I think. He was a mighty man, knew his work and management and everything. I was managing Gulperan then—Aboriginal manager. Peter Hannath was the white-man manager. We had Peter Sherman to make a yard here.

Peter Hannath wasn't a bad bloke but you know, he didn't really have a lot of respect for Aboriginal people, old people. In that Gulperan time, I had a lot of time for Peter. He had a few arguments with the Aborigines and I was an Aborigine too. But he was a man that you can rely on. I had a lot of time for him, because he helped me all the while.

He helped us to get more money. He used to go uphill and down till we went right over the hill in getting more money from ABTF to get more cattle, horses, saddles, like riding gear and all that. He used to do the book works and things like that. He was a mighty man, a reliable fellow. For instance, we wanted cattle. We had plenty of cattle here, but we wanted good breeders to restock our breeding herd. So we bought, I think, about nearly two thousand head of cattle. We had good Brahman bulls and good Brahman cows and cross breeds and all that, from different places.

We used to brand about six hundred calves every year and sell a few stock you know, a few steers, maybe a hundred and fifty or two hundred and we bought some horses from here and there.

Peter Hannath, manager for Gulperan (1975)

We never had any houses or things like that. Western Nuclear mining mob left a lot of gear here, and that was the only houses we had, but we had yards built and sixty miles of fencing. And in a few years we had nearly twenty five hundred head of cattle, from breedings and from the ones we used to muster from outside of this area. There were well over two thousand head, in this country. We just sold a few every year.

Then well, we had that money for Gulperan cattle station. Me and Peter Hannath, we fought all the way to get that money. It took us a couple of years of going downhill and uphill before we eventually went uphill. We got some money, so we were flying everywhere buying cattle. Breeder bulls, first class Brahman bulls and Santa Gertrudis from Queensland and all over the place. We had close on two thousand head of cattle. We could be sitting here and cattle right round us. Boy it was great. We wanted a contract to build all the fences. Peter Schubert came down and did all that, sixty miles of fencing. It's all broken down now, wires all over the place. He built that steel yard there. We used to brand about six hundred calves every year and sell a few cattle.

After we got all that money, we were finished up after that. By that time Peter Hannath and me were struggling for money to keep going. We went bankrupt.

That was when I left. I was already six years a manager here and it started to get stale. My wages was always on because I was the blackfella manager while

Peter Hannath was the whitefella manager. I knew it was going to go backwards, because the abattoirs left. We tried again to get some money but Gulperan went bankrupt after Peter Hannath left. We couldn't pay him because the government stopped the funding. They couldn't give us any more money and we was going to live off the stock that we sell.

Then Milton Hayes came up, and he didn't want me as manager, he wanted an Aboriginal manager so he can rip them off. He used to buy second hand video players and sell them for six hundred dollars when they only cost around three hundred dollars. So I ended up working back at Mainoru again for a year or so.

When I left Milton Hayes told everybody he had sacked me. Willy Martin said to him 'Why did you sent Tex away? We don't want you here, you're a rip off.' Willy sacked him on the spot! So he left in twenty-four hours.

After I left they had Aboriginal managers then. Rex Campion was manager and he sold cattle, then after that Bruce Murray was manager and then he died. He was a good man but didn't know the cattle like I did. Rex was a cattle man.

I had been managing Gulperan all that time; I managed for nearly nine years you know. Finally they said well, I had to give another fellow a chance. Bruce Murray took it over for manager then. And afterwards, after he died, all the cattle got out, broke the fences, just left. They went all over the place, Mainoru and everywhere.

My wishes are all finished now, what I was going to do. It could still be a cattle station but some of these Bulman boys say it's too hard to chase the cattle around, the cattle are all spoilt now. It would take good horses, a Phar Lap to catch up with them. They might come quiet if there were good boys who could be stockmen. It could still work out.

They started drinking. I used to send them out fencing and they'd sleep and play cards. When Peter Hannath was here, and I said I was going into town, I said go out at eleven o'clock and see what they doing. He went out and found they were sleeping and playing cards. And it went down, down, down. They did a little bit of work till eleven o'clock and then they'd come back for the issue of three cans [of beer].

Managers

Both Rex and Bruce were young Aboriginal men who had to deal with the funding guidelines of the Department of Aboriginal Affairs (DAA) as conveyed by state officials as well as with the changing prices of the beef market. When Rex independently arranged for cattle to be mustered and sold he was reprimanded by the DAA officials for not consulting with them first. They were concerned that he might not get the best price but Rex was angry and humiliated by this experience. Bruce died in a vehicle accident while he was manager.

When I left the fence were neglected, all broken down. Cattle nearly two thousand head just walked out. When I found out I didn't know what to say, after all that work. When you came up, cattle was on the road, not good to see. After I left well, there were different managers then. Oh, they robbed the Aborigines blind. I was so disappointed that I left and worked at Mainoru then, back to the old station where I started from. Kevin Analzark was manager of Mainoru then. I worked there for quite a while and Nelly come up there and we worked there for three months, me and Rexie. Mainoru used to send their young store steers for adjistment here to Bulman. When they grow up, we used to muster and send the young steers to sell to the butchers there and make money for Mainoru.

28. THE SADDLERY

I came back here to Bulman again after that. Saddlery business came up when somebody, bloke that knew me for twenty years, a Council man from Borroloola, said 'why don't you start saddlery'. I said to myself it might be a good time for me to work and I went there to have a meeting. He was telling everyone how I rode a buckjumper in Mainoru. He was the one that helped me really. There was a committee for ABTA [Aboriginal Benefit Trust Account] and saddlery gear was the first thing I asked for. I didn't ask for much. I asked for twenty five thousand, if I could get saddlery gear for these trainees you know, after they finish with Kormilda school or with Batchelor College. They come back straight into the saddlery job, instead of loafing around the camp there, doing nothing.

> **Education**
>
> After primary school at Bulman, the children can board at Kormilda College in Darwin, which until recently catered mainly for Aboriginal secondary school students from the top end of the Northern Territory. Batchelor College is where they can train as teachers, health workers or gain a general tertiary education.

When we went to Darwin for a full Council meeting, they put me as executive. I talked to the Council about trying to start a saddle business going. After that the executives had a meeting with the ABTA, and I was one of them, so me and a few others, we talked about it. He poked me in the ribs, this bloke and said, 'Now you'd better try and ask for some money.' So I asked them and I got quite a bit of money.

Well they said, 'That's a good business you know.' So they gave me something around twenty-six thousand dollars for all that equipment and that shed. I'm going to teach them young people how to make the saddles and mend them and all that.

Then we had to wait until I could get the orders and start buying. Then away we went. The next year I tried again and they couldn't give me any money until after the wet season, so I went broke, closed the saddlery. I kept asking and eventually they said 'You've got some money now, do you want to start up again?' So I started up again. I got all the leathers and things I wanted, made about three thousand dollars. I didn't use that much, not for anything else but leather work. So me and Peter Sherman went to Darwin. We bought this, bought that. We used the money on saddlery stuff, not for anything else. I'm waiting for a sewing machine for leather, saddles. It's a tricky job, I've still got a lot to learn about it because I've never used one before. When it comes out I might have to go to Darwin and work with other machinists to learn about it. They've got about three or four places that made wallets, swag covers and things like that. I'll be able to make stuff like that now.

That Thunderbolt mining mob, they came up to talk about this house of Nelly's and my saddle shed. If they find a mineral deposit they're going to come around here to dig it out. If it's a big one, they'll ask Nelly if they can buy this and build her another house where she wants it. They'll probably give her a generator I suppose, and all that. It's worth a lot of money, this house. They said we can still stay here, but that's no good with dynamite going and machines going day and night.

If they decide to get my saddle shed, well my saddle shed cost about twenty-eight or twenty-nine thousand. I'd get the money and build it somewhere away from here. But there's no place for me. If I go to Mary Lake, that belongs to someone else's country and they'll be wanting money. I'll share the money to them. The only other place I can go back to is Roper, or down Bigetti. I can't build it this side of the river because it's Dowani. They'll want a bit of that money too. I just don't know where to go.

The only thing I can think of is I could go back to Urapunga or Bob's Yard, Damareri, Wangalara—that's my tribal country. It joins up to Urapunga, and north of that it goes up to Wangalara. Damareri. We're talking about Wangalara, they reckon it's good for tourism, lot of rocks, waterholes, a few paintings.

> **Homelessness**
>
> Tex' sense of homelessness can be attributed partly to the interruptions in his attachments to traditional country due to his removal as a child, schooling at Groote Eylandt and at Roper, and to his work as a stockman.
>
> But the recognition of land rights and native title has also allowed traditional owners to assert the rights that had been denied since Europeans arrived and this has meant the questioning of more recent attachments such as Tex' link with the cattle stations and with Bulman.

29. YOUNG PEOPLE

Left hand kangaroo, that's my totem. See I'm the boss, like I'm a culture man. That's like a foundation structure. They call me a big boss today, even the Ngukurr mob, Ramingining, Maningrida, Yirrkala, even Oenpelli. I'm the King. Like I'm not exaggerating, that's the way. Like Sam Bulangan, Sam Thompson, from Ngukurr. He was my boss too, my teacher and I'm the boss now, the teacher you know.

In my days, especially down in Roper, we were in the old missions together. They'd learn about the old people and keep the culture going. Some are still fighting for their culture all the time. They worry about how the young people will carry on. It's a shame to see the young people chasing card games and petrol sniffers. They can't work for their mother or aunty or uncle. The old people are gonna die out. The family doesn't improve when they come out from education. They've got the best education, not like me, I didn't have education at all. They used to belt me round the flat and make me go into school. Aboriginal teachers, half-caste teachers. It wasn't good enough. They've got top notch teachers now. We had it rough, really rough. I don't know how we went through. I can read and write but I can't sit in the office and do those things.

But when people are drunk they don't know what they talking about. The young people just upset us old people. The old timers like Chuckaduck, Dick and Larry. We were trying to get to their brains to change their way of living, because they've got a culture and they don't use it the right way. Same thing everywhere, Ngukurr, Maningrida, Milingimbi. The old people are dying out and I don't think the young people should take over.

Country

The country everywhere has immense and complex significance in Aboriginal law. Every area is the responsibility of a clan group with its *Djungaii,* ceremonies and designs. Working out the details of these responsibilities is an ongoing preoccupation among Aboriginal people. There are constant negotiations about the exact rights and responsibilities of individuals in relation to specific places and significant sites.

Djungaii are the managers and performers of particular ceremonies. The roles are reciprocal, so that a person who is a manager for a *Gunabibi* ceremony will be a performer in *Yabuduruwa*. The ceremonies thus affirm the interdependence of segments of the population within the overall law.

The old people are frightened that they might sell all that what we use in the ceremony. That'll cost millions and millions of dollars. If some *Djungaii* is still alive they might crack it on the head and kill him altogether. They no good to this country now these young people.

A lot of young people, they just know nothing. All they do is driving around the country. They even pinch tyres and they running around all over the place. We give them the ceremony to hold it, because we are going to die. They just laugh about it. We showing that it's good, the ceremony side. They should hold it, try to sit like old people, sit down at the campfire and talk about it. They not doing the right thing by the law and those old people that are trying to give them the law. What are they going to do? If they do wrong things they'll get their problems anyhow. There's a lot of people that died over these things.

That's the downfall of the young people now. They don't realise themselves when they go to Batchelor College, or Kormilda or Saint Johns College in Darwin, or Slade up in Queensland. They pass the exams and when they come back they can't even work. All the education that has been given to them, to keep the place going for all the old Aboriginal people, their mother and father. They've lost their culture now. There's not too many old people here. Some of the old people still carry on the culture, the old people like Smiler Martin and Hitler Katcharelli and myself. They worry what they're going to do when they all die, whether they're going to keep the culture on or not.

When they come out here, when they've been at Batchelor or Kormilda or Saint Johns for education, they can't do it, they're lost. It would be all right if they put a big Aboriginal place in Darwin to do the papers and book work and things and keep the Arnhem Land going and keep the white man out from here, especially white men that don't like Aboriginal people, so they can keep the culture going, fight for that all the time. They can go back to Darwin again and come down to ceremonies when they're on. But they've just lost it. As soon as they're out from here they forget about those things. They come back some of them pregnant, no father, it's terrible.

Aboriginal law is still here. Those things, they find out. They can't just go ahead and leave problems behind, sort of bridging it, instead of starting off at the start. That girl here was killed because she was using a frying pan—just a frying pan for meat. Well the old people say that belonged to this old fella at Ngukurr. When he died all his

---

Death and its causes

This young woman was killed at Bulman. The perpetrator has been arrested, tried and convicted. However, the victim's family has a sense that other forces must have been at work to cause the death, and some more comprehensive explanation to do with the ordering of the world is sought.

things were supposed to go back to a certain lot of people, not young people. They've got to go through a bit of a ceremony to make that frying pan useable by anybody. Apparently she used the frying pan before it was clean [purified]. Everybody says it was over that. But some people reckon it's for something else that happened that got this girl in Bulman.

So maybe in the long run they will find out which way it went. Aboriginal people, they're just like detectives, they'll go right back and follow it up. It's going that way now, whether they're gonna let that bloke who killed her out of gaol. I think they're going to put him in for life because there's problems in the background. When they find out when the court case is going on, somebody might talk about who is the murderer. That bloke stabbed her, he's the murderer, but they've got to look in the background. There's something else behind it. We all know he's the murderer, but they'll find the real source from the frying pan.

30. GODS

Aboriginal people are Gods themselves.

Like, 'thou shall not steal, thou shalt not commit adultery'. Well Aboriginal people have got that too. Same law.

But some scientists say that the Aboriginal God made that country. I can say *Wullungurru* [ancestral spirit] made that country, or catfish, or snake dreaming. They made that. You can't go and just put yourself in there unless you find out from *Djungaii*. If there's a true God he'll know about it. They reckon he's everywhere, God.

You go in every settlement they'll tell you the same thing. Sacred sites, sacred trees grow up, and anthills. God made them. That's why we preserve them. That's our dreaming. Well Aboriginal people should take it over, take over the land. Europeans just go hell west and crooked, 'Oh that's nothing, we'll get that tree and just plant over it.'

It's not like that. That tree stays there and stays there.

These hills and things like that. That's dreaming country. God made it. But we don't know what God is. I believe in Jesus Christ, but we don't know where's God. I never see it. The only thing I can accept is that God is in Aboriginal people. He can come and destroy us, everyone.

That's the same law as the bible, the Aboriginal people carry on that.

Tex Camfoo at Bulman (1999)

I just go by the Bible, Genesis, that God made the land, trees and hills, Adam and Eve, from one of the rib bones I think. He made him and he was alive and he thought, I'll get a company for him, and he broke another rib and made Eve. And he gave them a good place, the Garden of Eden. Then the old snake went and tempted Eve. God told them not to touch this holy tree and don't eat any apples. The old snake, that is Satan now, had to come up and tempt them. He said, 'That's only *gaman* [pretend] now. If you eat that apple you'll live forever'.

So Eve pulled one off and eat it and said, 'We've got to eat it.'

'No we can't eat it. It's holy, it's sacred.'

But he did, then everything went wild. And they found themselves naked and pulled branches, *jut jut* [the Arnhem Land bark equivalent of a fig leaf] to wear that because they were naked. And animals went wild. And trees, you could eat any wild apples and plums. Everything went poison.

That's why I always think that Aboriginal people know that. When God said this place belongs to you mob, but that tree is sacred, you can't eat this plum you can't eat this berry and this and that, I think then maybe Aboriginal people were God. In the back of my mind, I think everyone come to that way of thinking now. That's why now Aboriginal people say, you can't touch that tree, that's dreaming tree and you can't dig hole there and everywhere. God made this country and left it for Aboriginal people to look after, that's the way I look at it.

In Council meetings a few years back I would say I think of that Aboriginal people are God. You know who told me that? One pommy chap, he used to pilot Eddy Connolan's planes before. Every fortnight they used to fly around stations taking the mail out to them. Fred Hogden, who used to be at Alice Springs. I said to him one time, 'Hey, they reckon you can't see God.'

'I'll tell you something', he said. 'God was a blackfella. He got black skin.'

And that's what woke me up then. Going back to the first part, Genesis. You work out whether they was white man or black man, Adam and Eve. God said you look after that country, the animals and that, but don't touch that tree, that's the tree of life. Eve made a mistake and God punished Eve. You will have your period every month. And you man, you will always work on the farm, sweating and drinking your own sweat. That's your punishment.

8. WOMEN'S CENTRE

Then [in the 1980s] I went to women's centre meetings in Lake Bennett and Pine Creek. DAA [Department of Aboriginal Affairs] and ADC [Aboriginal Development Corporation] gave money for the women's centre [place where women gather to learn skills of various kinds]. First we set it up with all the women chucking in twenty dollars and we bought the food and made money with that. I had to cook outside for three months because the contractor was still building the cooking place. I went into the bank and I got a shock that I had seven thousand dollars in there. Then DAA were really interested and they chucked a lot of money to us. Well it came on top [was successful]. We were employed by DEET [Department of Education, Employment and Training] and then we went on our own.

I'm going to retire, and let the younger girls run the business. I won't be here all the time, because ceremony is all around and I'm a business lady. But the reason I wanted this women's centre was to make a lively station for these young people to work. When they're maybe twenty years old or seventeen years old or eleven years old, when they come back from Kormilda College, they can come up and work and make money to go back to Kormilda or Batchelor College or anywhere. What I am trying to do is to keep the country going good and keep the money going good for the long term.

It's a pity I didn't go to school like you. I might be an Aboriginal Welfare lady now.

> **Business lady**
>
> 'Business' refers to ceremony, and a business lady is one who has important responsibilities to manage and perform ceremonial duties. But Nelly is also a women's representative on the Northern Territory's Heritage Commission and is combining the meanings of 'business lady' from both the white and black realms.

Nelly Camfoo (1991)

Photo: Hal Wootten

9. I DIDN'T GET MY CULTURE FROM MR KEATING

This *Djarada* women's ceremony, it's life for us, body for us, culture for us. I've got to tell that Canberra mob to come down and have a look. I'll ask them, 'Did *you* give us this dance and ceremony and all that? Did *you* teach me this language? Did we get this land from you?'

We were born with our own culture. My great grandpa, great grandma, mother, uncle, everything, they were born first and when I was born *they* were teaching me culture. I didn't get it from Mr Keating or a school teacher. My teachers were my parents, and my culture was my teacher too. We can't ever have a meeting to change it. *Mununga* can change his culture, but us mob, we can't change ours. We stick to it all the time. We just hold one ceremony and one culture and one body.

This *Djarada* and *Murrdu* this is our life, our own life. That's the same life like your minerals and everything. If we all die, nothing could happen, because nobody else can follow this meaning, and nobody else can follow this culture.

Djarada is where spirit *munga munga* dance. *Murrdu* is another story again. It's a bit like *Djarada*, but if somebody wants to understand how we run our women's story and women's culture, then you can talk and show them how this *Murrdu* is. That's the one we can talk about, it's not secret. That *Djarada* it's properly secret one, sacred love song, nobody can look, nobody can listen. Man are not allowed to look. But we can tell you the story about that *Murrdu* now, say to the parliament. And you can even play the tape of that song and send some photo with it. And you can show how we

---

Australian politics and politicians

The community at Bulman became caught up in the politics surrounding Aborigines in the 1980s as governments debated and competed for policies which would solve problems without upsetting their electorates.

Paul Keating was Prime Minister in 1993 when Nelly made this recording.

Nelly is offended that these politicians do not accept that Aboriginal law is real and significant. Her sense of authority stems from her own knowledge of that law which is demonstrated in the performance of songs and ceremony, as well as in the kinship system. Every Aboriginal person's knowledge forms a part of the body of the law which is a mosaic of segments seen to lie across the country, and which is evident in its contours and characteristics.

keep women's culture tight. Like women's ceremony you know. They can look. Then we can prove it to the *mununga* you know, because some people don't believe it.

Murrdu and *Djarada*. It's like for you, you have those olden-time dances, and rock and roll, that's the new one. Well, by our law we say *Djarada* is the new one. Olden time dance, slow one, that one we call *Murrdu*. And you can sing that one, that's the one we can show to your colour, to *mununga*. The *Murrdu* you can dance for *mununga* now. Say when Professor Elkin [Professor of Anthropology at Sydney University] wanted to come and look, we put a *Murrdu* for him before, at Mainoru [in 1949].

When we're teaching our kids, first we doing it with *Murrdu* and then they come bigger and bigger and then they're learning the proper *Djarada*, that really sacred one. They were learning that last year when we did it. It is a different kind altogether from men's dances.

This *Djarada* and *Murrdu*, this is our life, this is our own life. Like men's business too, that's our life. That's the same life like minerals and everything for white people. If we are all going to be dead nothing can happen because nobody else can follow this meaning, and nobody else can follow this culture. They belong to it, this little young mob here. Maybe, if they are listening, and they are dancing, I hope they will carry on. This is the only women's ceremony, the only women's *Djarada*. It come from long time, long time. My great grandmother, and my grandmother and my aunty. My father's sister. They were teaching me when I was six years old, or like Susan was teaching the kids here. No clothes, teaching this way.

This *Djarada* belongs to Ngalakan and Rembarrnga. This hill here is for the full blood Ngalakan, Ngandu, and Rembarrnga come on top. This now is the only one place for this *Djarada*. That *munga munga*, it's our mother you know, for all of us. The *Djungaii*, bosses for that ceremony, they've got two kinds of skin. They are *Wamutjan* and *Ngaritjan* [skin or subsection names]. This old woman, *Bulangan* here is the nana, *gokgok* [grandmother], of the *munga munga*. We've got *Dua* and *Yirritja* country.

Country

Dua and *Yirritja* are the two moieties, representing two fundamental categories into which all people, ceremonies, plants, songs are divided. The eight subsections or 'skins' are further divisions of the moieties. Similar kinds of divisions and categories are used right across Australia, so that Aboriginal people can relate to others from distant areas and know who they should call 'sister' and who 'uncle' and so on. This extending of family relationships is known as 'classificatory' kinship among anthropologists.

But that *Murrdain* [men's ceremony], women can't look at that one. Men can look, but they not allowed to put it in a book otherwise white women might look. It's just the same for white women, because they are women, and if they read it, they lose their life, just the same as we. For *Murrdain*, and *Gunabibi* and *Yabuduruwa*.

Other tribe can fit in with our tribe's *Djarada*. Like Yarralin. I think they got *munga munga*. Alice Spring side they've got *munga munga* too. We were asking them, 'You mob got a different *munga munga* than us. How come?' It sounds different, the way they talk, but it fits in somehow.

10. VOTING

'We want to open a ceremony, a *Gunabibi* or a *Yabuduruwa* up here.'

That's what the bosses say, the *Djungaii* and *Mingeringi* [managers and owners of ceremonies]. And they come up and tell women's *Djungaii* and *Mingeringi*. 'Well, we are going to start putting on a ceremony now to take back my father's shadow, or my uncle's shadow.' That shadow has to go back to that ceremony.

That's what we do. We don't vote for anyone. Like that election coming up, what's it for? We don't like elections. They belong to *mununga*. The whitefella might say, 'It's too late now, you have to come in my law.' If he says that I've got to say, 'You can't change my mind. You've got your own mind. I've got my own mind. My own brains tell me what to do. Like my brains tell me which way to go, left or right.'

> **Mortuary ritual**
>
> The 'shadow' or 'spirit' of a dead person is returned to its country through the rituals which take place during ceremonial events. [see Howard Morphy, *Journey to the Crocodile's Nest*, 1984]

When there's an election, we vote for all the *mununga* in Canberra. We're silly I reckon, but we have to vote because we've got that police law. We are citizens now. We've got policemen all around the blackfella, but we are in the middle. But we can't ever change our culture. You see?

I will vote but I'll never win. That's white law. We just vote, we don't get anything out of it. I can vote for some bloke, but maybe I'm voting for a bad man who will bring war to Arnhem Land. I vote because I'm in *mununga* country now. If I don't vote, poor old lubra me, I'll get a summons letter, and I'm fined fifty dollar or whatever it is. And if I don't pay I'll go to gaol. That's your *mununga* rule. So I have to vote while I'm here wearing your clothes and talking your English and smoking your tobacco, eating your sugar and tea, and talking to your tape recorder. It's not the blackfella way!

We just had a letter stick us mob. And for Toyota, we had our foot. That foot was walking a long way. We walked to Roper, and took the ceremony to

Maningrida from Bulman. We would go easy, slowly with our *Dutji* [sacred object], ceremony *Dutji*, the big business sacred one. It's like your bomb, that *Dutji*. If we go rough with it, it might blow up. We would take maybe one week, two weeks, three weeks. Now everybody has a Toyota, but they roll over and people die. The *mununga* way has spoiled it, you see. And yet the government reckons they can make all this law, and if we talk, the government says we are *gaman* [lying].

Why don't they just believe our word instead of taking us in the court [Land Courts]? Canberra people know we are living here. If they are talking about Arnhem Land, they should come and talk to us here like Senator Richardson. We are close to Darwin and the Darwin mob. Steve Hatton should understand Arnhem Land people and come up and talk to us. But those *mununga* come up and brainwash Aboriginal people. We tell them from our own mouth, but they still can't understand what we are doing. One man, like a field officer, he takes it back to that meeting, to his parliament. But he didn't understand or else he doesn't pass it on. Only people who stay and listen can know.

Land Rights

Land Courts were set up in the Northern Territory after *the Aboriginal Land Rights (NT) Act 1976*. Aboriginal traditional owners have to demonstrate their ownership to the satisfaction of the Land Commissioner before they can be given rights to the country claimed.

Australian politics and politicians

Graham Richardson visited Bulman in 1994 as Minister of Health in the Australian Labor government.

Steve Hatton was Chief Minister in the Northern Territory Country Liberal Party Government from 1986–88. He subsequently held various other Ministries, including Aboriginal Development in the mid 1990s.

11. WE DUSTED THEM UP

When Bob Hawke and his wife came to Barunga they were bright and shiny, really clean, from Canberra. 'Oh here's Bob Hawke', and everybody stood up.

Goodness, when they stayed with us, we dusted them up! We were dancing and we dusted them two up properly. When corroboree was finished I was chucking my eye [looking] to where that Bob Hawke is. I couldn't see him! I saw something just like a bull come out of the ground, from bull dust, poorfella! Because his hair was grey and the shirt was all dusty. His missus looked worse. When the corroboree was finished they went back to the motel in Katherine where they had booked their room. They were really like pigs, properly really dusty one poorfella.

> **Australian politics and politicians**
>
> Australian Prime Minister Bob Hawke visited Barunga for the annual festival in 1988 and signed a 'Makarata' or treaty with the local Aboriginal people.

That's the kind of man that was interested in us. Maybe he learned from us. He might have believed it, I don't know. And Bob Hawke—his boomerang won't come back! He tried and that boomerang just went forward and missed that kangaroo, that toy kangaroo. And his wife, she went round and look around how we doing mats, making them from pandanus leaf.

When he was doing that, maybe that put something in his head. They finished throwing spear and he went along and looked at the dancing. He saw six different dances, from everywhere. From Lajamanu and from desert country, all different places. He sat down from morning time close up to two o'clock. Might be that man had close up heart attack where he saw a lot of different cultures. I don't know if he was frightened, or if he is still saying that we telling lies, that we making that culture up. I don't know. I'd like to know if it proves what we do in our own culture.

But that has all passed now. He was really happy and he shook hands with me too, that Bob Hawke. Holding out his finger. *Mununga* finger was there and blackfella finger was there, together. That's the kind of man we want to come down here.

Paul Keating or his office should come down, or his bookkeeper or whatever he is, to visit to Top End and tell us where we are going to stay for ceremony, to pick our ceremony area. They only going to find it by *us* telling *them*. They don't know where we are. Even policeman can't know where we are. They make all the decision themselves but they don't know what we are doing.

We like to be interested too, seeing we are in a *mununga* place now.

12. MONEY IN STONES

Those *mununga* who came down, say to Beswick station and Barunga and all that, or Mountain Valley station, nearly all the *mununga* came down to blackfella country. We don't go out to whitefella country. We can't go as far as Sydney or Adelaide or whatever, or to London or wherever people live. We can't even go to Hong Kong. There's a lot of Chinamen around here in Australia in our country. So we look silly. Us mob of blackfella look silly when whitefella come over and take all the country from us. For instance especially Mainoru and Mountain Valley. So white men take country from us. Why is that? Why?

Yes, it's because we're rich, up here we're rich. Tiger Brennan had a silver lead mine there for a long time. All them Ngalpon mob, you know all them Dalapon people they worked there. All the different companies mining for manganese and diamonds, they came up and asked us this time. We didn't want all that. We told them we don't want any mining. We were born with bush tucker, we were born on the ground. We never wore clothes before, we didn't know the wireless, we didn't even know about motor cars. We are just learning. We don't want that mining.

We have lived here for forty thousand years. We used to walk over pretty stones [coloured rock formations], with lead or diamond. We still know where that stone is. The snake made that stone, and big kangaroo made some, and goanna made them. We say it is goanna *guna* [droppings], kangaroo *guna*, snake

Nelly Camfoo at Bulman (1999)

guna, and that was made out of our own body, our own culture. We didn't know rocks had money in them, or that money can come out of those rocks. *Mununga* call it lead or diamond or silver-lead and they know there's money there. Mining people want to come up and dig all that up, so we might lose our life. If other people don't kill us [for not protecting the country] we can get sick from that stone. We are going to be sick and the doctor won't know what's wrong. Doctor can't understand blackfella way.

They say that mining can make a person rich. Only the mining boss himself is rich. But mining is ruining our place. If that mining is in a ceremony area, that's our body they are busting up. They are digging our body and grinding it up in that machine and hurting our feelings. All that stone with the dots, that's our culture. That's the snake's *guna*. I am snake dreaming too, and the mining makes us mob sick.

Mununga does not understand that because *mununga* says, 'that's money'. He makes himself rich and he can't give anything to others, to blackfellas. Some of them will go fifty-fifty with the *mununga*. But these mining people here, they only give to traditional owner. It's not fair. We *all* own that snake *guna* dreaming. That's everywhere. Coronation Hill, Jabiru, Pine Creek and Gove too and Groote Island.

We should all get the money. Whole lot of us, *Djungaii*.

Now I'll tell you something funny.

Mabo

Mabo refers to the High Court decision in 1992 which found that native title does exist in Australia, thus overturning the doctrine of *terra nullius* [unoccupied land] which had been the legal basis of previous dealings with land.

What we call *mabo* is when people chew tobacco. When we heard that they had a meeting in Canberra or somewhere talking about *mabo* I said to people, 'Hey! They're giving us a new rule not to chew tobacco!'

And they said, 'No, I heard they had meeting in Canberra about changing the law for *mabo* and we've *all* got to chew that black tobacco now!'

All right. So another meeting comes along for Mabo. But what does that Mabo mean? What's Mabo got to do with us mob here in Arnhem Land? What's it got to do with me? Where's that Mabo coming from? It didn't come from blackfella.

REFERENCES

Cowlishaw, G., 1999, *Rednecks, Eggheads and Blackfellas: a study of racial power and intimacy in Australia*, Allen & Unwin, Sydney.

Cumming, B., 1990, *Take This Child: from Kahlin Compound to the Retta Dixon Children's Home*, Aboriginal Studies Press, Canberra.

Dewar, M., 1992, *The Black War in Arnhem Land: Missionaries and the Yolngu 1908–1940*, Australian National University, Canberra.

Egan, T., 1997, *Sitdown Up North*, Kerr Publishing, Sydney.

Elkin, A.P., 1997, *Aboriginal Men of High Degree*, Inner Traditions, Vermont.

Lockwood, D., 1962, *I, the Aboriginal,* Rigby, Adelaide.

—— 1964, *Up the Track*, Rigby, Adelaide.

McGrath, A., 1987, *Born in the Cattle*, Allen & Unwin, Sydney.

Morphy, H., 1984, *Journey to the Crocodile's Nest*, Australian Institute of Aboriginal Studies, Canberra.

Mudrooroo, 1995, *Us Mob: History, culture, struggle: an introduction to Indigenous Australia*, Angus & Robertson, Sydney, New York.

POSTSCRIPT

Heather Dodd inherited Mainoru station when Jack McKay died in 1968. But since it was in debt and award wages had to be paid to Aboriginal station workers, Heather sold it soon afterwards and the community which had been established there since the 1920s was forced to leave over the next two years.

The Gulperan Pastoral Company, which Tex was so enthusiastic about when it began in 1972, was a project of the newly formed Department of Aboriginal Affairs (DAA) under the new policy of self-determination for Aboriginal communities. Enterprises were funded with the intention of making communities economically independent. There was little recognition among the well-meaning bureaucrats of the pitfalls of establishing a pastoral project on economically marginal country with inexperienced managers who were also sometimes incompetent or dishonest. Gulperan was also supposed to be a community development project run by the community itself. But while many at Bulman were skilled and experienced stockworkers, no-one knew about either bureaucratic or business matters. Indeed most of the Rembarrnga adults were illiterate and innumerate.

After 1977 the DAA officials confessed to the failure of the project, and admitted that it should have been managed differently. The station then became a low-key cattle and buffalo harvesting project. The bureaucrats of this era strongly supported self-determination, but unlike the McKays and Dodds of Mainoru station, they did not know anything about the traditions or the historical experience of Nelly and Tex and the whole community.

Some Rembarrnga people returned to Mainoru station after 1977 because the new manager Kevin Analzark was friendly and supportive. Further there was some schooling available, taught by Nelly's niece Annette Murray, who had attended secondary school at Kormilda College in Darwin. She began to teach the children regularly but the request from the manager that she be paid was turned down because the school was not registered and Annette was not then a trained teacher. Such rules of course make sense in the white world, but to Annette it was a rejection of her worth. She subsequently studied at Batchelor College and Deakin University and is now a fully qualified teacher.

In 1981 Mainoru was again sold and the departing manager warned the DAA that the new owner 'was not favourably disposed towards Aboriginal people.' The more typical Territory style of management re-emerged. Instead of employing the Bulman stockmen, the new owner brought in Aboriginal workers from Mataranka, provided for them on the station, and delivered them back, wages in hand, when the muster was completed. This represented another severance of Rembarrnga people from Mainoru station where many of them had been born and where some had worked since they were small children and where family members had been buried.

Since 1976 the material conditions of the 140 or so Bulman residents have altered greatly. Tex and Nelly have a house at the old camp, Gonjimbi, and have their own vehicle. A town has been constructed at the new site of Gulin Gulin where there had been grass, stony red earth and a symbolic landscape of dreaming tracks and sites. Each year improved housing and facilities have been built including a generator, a clinic, a mobile school in 1977 and a permanent two room school in 1995. After years of inadequate, overflowing septic tanks, a proper sewerage treatment plant has been installed. There are four wheel drive vehicles, mostly owned by organisations or supplied to staff by a government department, and an all weather road to Katherine. A few residents have unregistered cars used for bush travel and kept going by the ingenuity of their owners. Buildings and equipment are evidence that the Bulman mob has participated, willy nilly, in the inexorable encroachment of modernity.

Self-determination was intended to mean that Aborigines would at once take over the running of their communities and develop commercial enterprises. At Bulman in the 1970s the common view was that those girls and boys away at college would be able to 'do the paper work' and thus whitefellas would be no longer required. Some skills were quickly acquired. But self-determination entails running the Council and understanding the constitution of incorporated bodies, the rules of organisations and accountability procedures. That is, the community has to manage itself in the same way as other white towns. Rembarrnga staff cannot easily introduce Rembarrnga practices into these activities. However, a community member is the elected Chairperson of Gulin Gulin Council, and several members of the community now have training and skills to do some of the more significant jobs of maintenance of equipment.

While community members have further schooling and some of the jobs, there are ever more whitefellas needed to staff the organisations and institutions. None of these staff stay very long. There are one or two Aboriginal staff with urban backgrounds. Young people from the community who have been encouraged to board at college in Darwin in the fond hope they could 'do the bookwork' for the community have, at most, junior, unskilled jobs. The accountant, store manager, bookkeeper, resource association manager and the senior staff of the school and clinic are all white.

Some aspects of life for remote Aboriginal communities are more comfortable and independent than they were in the 'blacks camps' on cattle stations. But independence and self-determination is often a facade which conceals a new invasion of all kinds of bureaucratic complexities which have created new frustrations and new forms of dependence and humiliation at the hands of whites. Tex and Nelly know little of the furious arguments at a national level about the ever changing government policies which affect them in complex ways as they struggle to come to grips with changing policies, changing personnel and changing cultural conditions.

The increased access to vehicles, planes and telephones in recent years has also made for changes in the relationship with the country compared with the days of 'footwalking'. Planes pluck people out of one community into another in minutes and visits to attend funerals, ceremonies or meetings need last only hours. Cars rush through the landscape without time to absorb and understand the moods and meanings of country. Many young people have not walked over the land with which their grandparents were intimately familiar. Further, while footwalking was available to all, vehicles are not equally distributed. Private ownership and varied incomes mean that the educated and employed men and women have access to more resources than their kin, creating new forms of interdependence and new inequalities within Aboriginal communities.

Nelly and Tex both take their responsibilities seriously in this era of increased interaction with institutions of the state. But the rules of meetings and bureaucratic procedures often seem irrational and inflexible. It seems that Rembarrnga notions of time, place and human interaction have to be modified to harmonise with the relatively inflexible rules. The school and the clinic are funded and controlled directly by government departments which ensure they continue to function within the framework of standard practice. There is often discord between social responsibility and the personal and family responsibilities which a kin based society practices in everyday interpersonal interchanges and interdependencies. The need to deal with funding budgets, town plans, census forms and employment programs, has brought about a situation where loyalty to community organisations is in competition with loyalty to kin. Clan identity and the law can be a rival with a modern community identity on some occasions.

Bulman has been able to recruit Aboriginal staff from among the 'stolen children', those light skinned children who were taken from their mothers and sent away to a 'half-caste establishment'. Ironically many have been able to return to their parents and kin as employees of the state which, in an earlier era, removed them. When Australian governments created and enforced a gulf between blackfellas and whitefellas, brown children fell into the gulf. For years they were expected to climb out on the white side but after 1970 state officials encouraged them to identify with their black relations. They are now accorded a valued place on the contemporary racial frontier in the role of liaising between their birth families and white institutions.

As the stories of both Nelly and Tex demonstrate, the connections between the children who were removed and their primary kin were not obliterated. The Bulman mob knew exactly who was taken and the sparse information about these absent children kept alive a social space for them to come back to. The chasm created by the racial conditions of the past is being bridged in many ways, providing dialogue between black and white Australians.

Gillian Cowlishaw